THIS IS

ISLAM

A Brief Guide to Islām's Foundations, Pillars and Obligations, its Morals and Ethics, its Position Towards Extremism and Terrorism and the Status of Women in Islām

قُلْ ءَامَنَّا بِٱللَّهِ وَمَآ أُنزِلَ عَلَيْنَا وَمَآ أُنزِلَ عَلَىٰٓ إِبْرَٰهِيمَ وَإِسْمَٰعِيلَ
وَإِسْحَٰقَ وَيَعْقُوبَ وَٱلْأَسْبَاطِ وَمَآ أُوتِىَ مُوسَىٰ وَعِيسَىٰ وَٱلنَّبِيُّونَ مِن
رَّبِّهِمْ لَا نُفَرِّقُ بَيْنَ أَحَدٍ مِّنْهُمْ وَنَحْنُ لَهُۥ مُسْلِمُونَ

Say: "We have believed in God (Allāh) and in what was revealed to us and what was revealed to **Abraham**, **Ishmael**, **Isaac**, **Jacob**, and **the Descendants**, and in what was given to **Moses** and **Jesus** and to **all the Prophets** from their Lord. We make no distinction between any of them, and we are Muslims [submitting] to Him."
The Qurʾān (3:84)

Abu ʿIyāḍ
Amjad bin Muḥammad Rafīq

Title: This is Islām
Author: Abū ʿIyāḍ Amjad bin Muḥammad Rafīq
Version: 2.30

2nd Edition, Safar 1441 AH / October 2019 CE

IslamAgainstExtremism.Com
@islamextremism

ISBN 13: 978-1-64467-302-7
ISBN 10: 1-64467-302-9

For further information contact:

Wright Street Mosque
472 Coventry Road
Small Heath
Birmingham B10 0UG
United Kingdom
t. +44 (0) 121 773 0033
e. admin@spubs.com

Germantown Masjid
4944 Germantown Avenue
Philadelphia
PA 19144
United States
t. +1 215 848 2615
e. admin@germantownmasjid.com

Masjid Bin Baz
East Road (next to no. 2)
Plaistow
London E15 3QR
United Kingdom
e. info@al-athariyyah.com

Masjid al-Furqan
874-A Weston Road
Toronto, Ontario
M6N 3R6, Canada
t. +1 416 243 5320
e. info@troid.ca

Masjid al-Sunnah
3 Paternoster Lane
Bradford BD7 3DS
United Kingdom
t. +44 (0) 1274 501 736
e. info@albaseerah.com

Muʿādh bin Jabal Centre
19 Spackmans Way
Slough, Berkshire
SL1 2SA
t. +44 (0) 1753 533376
e. info@markazmuaadh.com

Contents

Transliteration Table

Consonants

ء	ʾ	د	d	ض	ḍ	ك	k
ب	b	ذ	dh	ط	ṭ	ل	l
ت	t	ر	r	ظ	ẓ	م	m
ث	th	ز	z	ع	ʿ	ن	n
ج	j	س	s	غ	gh	هـ	h
ح	ḥ	ش	sh	ف	f	و	w
خ	kh	ص	ṣ	ق	q	ي	y

Vowels

Short	ـَ	a	ـِ	i	ـُ	u
Long	ـَا	ā	ـِي	ī	ـُو	ū
Dipthongs	ـَوْ	aw	ـَيْ	ay		

عَزَّوَجَلَّ	The Mighty and Majestic.
صَلَّىٱللَّهُعَلَيْهِوَسَلَّمَ	May Allāh make good mention of His Prophet in the highest company and grant him safety.
عَلَيْهِٱلسَّلَامُ	Peace be upon him.
رَضِيَٱللَّهُعَنْهُ	Allāh be pleased with him.

Disclaimer: It is impossible to translate the Qurʾān into any other language whilst retaining its full range and depth of meaning. Hence, all verses from the Qurʾān cited in this work, whilst providing an accurate enough rendition of the basic meaning, remain limited due to the limitations of the English language and are unable to convey fully what is in the original Arabic. **Note:** Parts of citations may appear with bolded or italicised text. This is from the author for purposes of emphasis.

Introduction

Dear respected reader,

Due to geopolitical events—*both past and contemporary*— there are many orientations that seek to portray Islām and Muslims in a negative light. These voices come from a wide range of ideological backgrounds and compete for your ears, heart and mind in order to shape opinions and fulfil agendas. It would be unfair to accept such ideologically motivated narratives without question and without giving Muslims a chance to:

- explain the reality of what they believe in and practise,
- free themselves from criminal acts perpetrated in their name,
- and explain the role which Islām plays in their lives.

The book in your hands offers a brief presentation of Islām for non-Muslims. It explains the most important foundations and pillars of Islām. It discusses the major obligations and prohibitions and the wisdoms behind them. Likewise, it covers morals and ethics in Islām and its position towards racism. It also discusses religious zeal, extremism and the activities of terrorists such as al-Qaeda, ISIS and similar groups. Finally, the book provides a brief treatment of women in Islām and addresses some common misconceptions related to this subject.

We hope it is both interesting and enlightening and serves as a stepping stone for a further objective and detailed study of Islām.

Abu ʿIyāḍ
19 Safar 1440
28 October 2018

Creation and Original Disposition (Fiṭrah)

We start our journey into the essentials of Islām with an affair that places all of humanity on the same footing, treating them as equals from birth. Known as the ***original disposition***, it refers to a natural inclination towards truth which if left intact predisposes a person towards Islām. Its explanation is as follows:

ଔ

In the teachings of the Prophets and Messengers of God[1], every child is born with an **ingrained subconscious acknowledgement** of a creator which forms part of its **original disposition.** Humans are also **hard-wired** to infer purpose and wisdom from basic reflection upon the observed order, regularity, contrivance, functionality and beauty of natural phenomena. In addition, all humans are endued with **a basic sense of morality** and the **anticipation of justice**. This explains the existence of a common, base set of morals between all people regardless of their ideas and beliefs about life and the universe. Collectively, all of this is referred to in Islām by the word **fiṭrah**, which means ***original disposition.*** It is the natural state upon which humans are born. If left alone without contrary teaching every child will go on to develop a natural desire to show gratitude to the Creator of whom he or she is *innately and intuitively* aware through the fiṭrah and then *perceptively* through the innumerable favours and bounties he or she experiences on a daily basis.

Due to this original disposition, humans are naturally inclined towards the message of the Prophets of God. To put it another way, humans are born **pure**, **innocent** and **predisposed towards truth and goodness**.

At birth, they are not inherently evil, nor guilty of sin, nor do they carry any burden on their shoulders. Nor are they considered inferior due to race, lineage, class or caste.

---

[1] The words for god in the languages of Hebrew, Aramaic (Syriac) and Arabic are *īl, el, ilāh, iloh, elah* and Allāh refers to the one, true deity. This is not "*the exclusive God of the Muslims*" but the God of all Prophets, Messengers and mankind. "God" has been used throughout this work to make for easier reading for a non-Muslim audience.

Alluding to this, God stated in the Qurʾān:

فِطْرَتَ اللَّهِ الَّتِي فَطَرَ النَّاسَ عَلَيْهَا لَا تَبْدِيلَ لِخَلْقِ اللَّهِ

"**The fiṭrah (natural state) [which] God (Allāh) determined and upon which He created [and moulded] mankind. Let there be no change in the creation of God**." (30:30).

And the Prophet Muḥammad (ﷺ) said: "*Every child is born upon the fiṭrah*."[2] The Prophet (ﷺ) also said, narrating from his Lord: "*I created My servants upright, inclined to truth (ḥunafāʾ).*"[3]

This fiṭrah is likened to a seed which has been planted in each soul, predisposing it to good. The message of Islām as conveyed by the Prophets of God appeals to the fiṭrah before it appeals to reason. With an uncorrupted fiṭrah a person is naturally inclined to the worship of God alone and **simply requires instruction and guidance** to nurture the fiṭrah to its full potential. The Muslim scholar Ibn Taymiyyah (d. 1328) stated: "The Messengers were sent to corroborate the fiṭrah and bring it to perfection."[4]

However, if this fiṭrah has been eroded, altered or corrupted—due to parents, society and environment—then the **faculty of reason** is appealed to in order to guide the instinct back to its original state. Thus, in conveying their messages, the Messengers of God appealed to the two human faculties of **original disposition (fiṭrah)** and **reason (ʿaql)**. In performing this task, they were instructed and guided by **revelation (waḥy)** from God.

The overwhelming majority of humans have never deviated from this natural tendency to believe in the existence of a creator and the desire to venerate and worship this creator. This tendency arises due to the original disposition, (fiṭrah), simple reflection upon the natural phenomena and inward acknowledgement that favours and benefits are being enjoyed. This establishes that this tendency is deeply ingrained and cannot be erased very easily because the factors giving rise to it are inescapable and universal.

In fact, in Arabic, the meaning of the root verb (faṭara) which is related to fiṭrah combines two concepts: that of ***creation, origination***

---

[2] Related by Muslim (no. 2658).
[3] Related by Muslim (no. 2865).
[4] Ibn Taymiyyah in *Amrāḍ al-Qulūb wa Shifāʾuhā* (p. 26).

and that of ***original state and disposition.*** The original state of humans is to recognise a creator, both innately and perceptively.

The entire input of all human perception and observation forces this inescapable conclusion and is one of the central arguments of the Qurʾān.

The Muslim scholar **Ibn al-Qayyim** (d. 1350) said: "Whoever reflects upon the whole universe, its upper and lower [parts] and all of its domains will find it bearing witness to the affirmation of its maker, originator and owner."[5]

In the 36th chapter of the Qurʾān (Yā Sīn), a story is told of a believer who sincerely pleads with the inhabitants of his city. They had already rejected a series of messengers sent to them. He said:

يَا قَوْمِ اتَّبِعُوا الْمُرْسَلِينَ اتَّبِعُوا مَن لَّا يَسْأَلُكُمْ أَجْرًا وَهُم مُّهْتَدُونَ وَمَا لِيَ لَا أَعْبُدُ الَّذِي فَطَرَنِي وَإِلَيْهِ تُرْجَعُونَ

---

[5] *Madārij al-Sālikīn* (1/82). Innate human faculties *unavoidably* generate beliefs of design, order and purpose which are rationally legitimate and warranted. Marks of design and purpose are recognized perceptually and implicitly (innately) and from here the inferential step to a designer is natural, minimal, rational and warranted. Such marks include contrivance, order, organization, intent, purpose, law-like behaviour, pursuit of goals or outcomes or goal-steering mechanisms, regularity, beauty and adaptation. This itself is the very source of the rational justification for science and the scientific method, since the scientific method has underlying assumptions that cannot be verified by the scientific method itself, and must be assumed. It is therefore not possible to separate innate beliefs about the universe from scientific inquiry and the scientific enterprise as a whole. This is why up until the 19th century, and in the entire history of humanity—with very rare exceptions—all scientific research was conducted by believers in a Creator on the basis that they were studying the mechanisms in creation—*the ways and means, the causes and effects, the handiwork of the Creator*—in order to gain further enlightenment about the Creator. Likewise, to exploit their findings to facilitate human progress. The entire scientific enterprise rests upon the assumptions that the universe is **real**, **material**, **orderly**, **designed**, **consistent** and **rationally investigable**. This is why it is impossible to erase the innate disposition (fiṭrah)—*in which belief in a Creator is permanently embedded*—through any amount of materialist brainwashing within the lifecycle of education. It is why people will always be inclined towards belief in God and the desire to worship a Creator. Detailed knowledge of that creator, however, can only come through the medium of revelation, and not any other means.

"O my people, follow the messengers. Follow those who ask you not for any payment and who are rightly-guided. And why should I not [be grateful and] worship the one who originated me (faṭaranī) and to whom you shall be returned?" (36:20-22).

The essence of the call of the Messengers of God is conveyed in the statement of this man. He employed the verb root (faṭara) and essentially said: "Why should I not be grateful and worship the one who originated me and everything around me and through whose immense creativity and power we subsist and enjoy tremendous, unending favours—*something both you and I feel innately and know perceptively through the physical senses?*"

This man appealed to the *original disposition* and the binding link between the observed *contrivance, order, functionality, regularity and beauty* in creation and what it generates of awe and the compelling desire to show gratitude to the Originator of creation.

Muslim scholars have explained the following statement of God in the Qurʾān in the same way:

قَالَتْ رُسُلُهُمْ أَفِي ٱللَّهِ شَكٌّ فَاطِرِ ٱلسَّمَٰوَٰتِ وَٱلْأَرْضِ

"Their messengers said: 'Is there any doubt about God (Allāh)? The Originator (Fāṭir) of the Heavens and Earth.'" (14:10).

There are two appeals made in this verse which summarises the call of the Messengers of God.

The first appeal is made to the fiṭrah, the original disposition, in which belief in a creator is firmly embedded. This is represented in the question, "**Is there any doubt about God (Allāh)?**", which implies—since His existence is not in doubt—that He alone is to be worshipped with gratitude and humility.

The second appeal is to observation, reflection and the use of reason. It addresses the situation where the original disposition has either been altered or buried with pride, arrogance or desires. This is represented in the statement, "**The Originator of the Heavens and Earth**", and requests observation, investigation and reflection upon God's creation—from which no other conclusion can be made except that the universe and all life therein were created with ***knowledge***, ***choice***, ***intent***, ***power*** and ***wisdom***. Thus, the Messengers appeal to the original disposition (fiṭrah) first as that is the default position in humanity, and thereafter, reason (ʿaql) based upon empirical evidence, should it be necessary.

Due to the very nature of the fitrah—*the innate, subconscious awareness of God*—and how it is **inseparably tied** to the observed design, contrivance, order and regularity of the universe—the very features giving rise to the assumptions required for undertaking any type of scientific investigation—**it is impossible for atheists to avoid terminology which presupposes design, purpose and wisdom in things.** This presupposition from which the fiṭrah is inseparable is the very foundation of all scientific inquiry. Despite this, atheists make a concerted and conscious effort to pretend otherwise and dismiss it all—quite arrogantly—***as mere illusion.*** On rare occasions, they are honest and frank enough to acknowledge the compelling feeling which overtakes them when they reflect upon creation and its wonders.

For example, in a debate about God's existence, atheist Richard Dawkins acknowledged: "I think that when you consider the beauty of the world and you wonder how it came to be what it is, you are naturally overwhelmed with a feeling of awe, a feeling of admiration and you almost feel a desire to worship something. I feel this... We, all of us, share a kind of religious reverence for the beauties of the universe, for the complexity of life. For the sheer magnitude of the cosmos, the sheer magnitude of geological time. And it's tempting to translate that feeling of awe and worship into a desire to worship some particular thing, a person, an agent. You want to attribute it to a maker, to a creator."[6]

This is the fiṭrah appealed to by the believing man mentioned earlier and appealed to by all the Messengers of God. Even the staunchest and most arrogant of atheists cannot escape this feeling on occasion, because it is latent and deep in the human soul. Disbelief (*kufr*) is when the natural expression of this fiṭrah—gratitude with the heart and limbs—is deliberately prevented or concealed due to arrogance and pride, or preference for lusts, or wealth, power, and authority. This disbelief may be rationalised thereafter, through claims about the origin of the universe and the

---

[6] As occurs in his Fixed-Point debate at the University of Alabama (2007) regarding his book "The God Delusion".

origin of life which are presented and packaged as scientifically validated truths. In reality, they are nothing but **conjectures** resting on ***hidden, undisclosed assumptions***, coupled with ***fallacious modes of logic and reasoning.*** [7]

Scientists are baffled and at a loss as to why—**despite sustained brainwashing with speculative materialist philosophy throughout the lifecycle of standard and higher education**—this natural tendency cannot be erased or blunted.[8] It is **God's "signature"** in His creatures, predisposing them to recognise Him and to worship Him alone.

From the above discussion, we can understand the previous statement of God in the Qurʾān:

فِطْرَتَ اللَّهِ الَّتِي فَطَرَ النَّاسَ عَلَيْهَا لَا تَبْدِيلَ لِخَلْقِ اللَّهِ

"**The fiṭrah (natural state) [which] God (Allāh) determined and upon which He created [and moulded] mankind. Let there be no change in the creation of God.**" (30:30). The Muslim scholar, **Imām al-Saʿdī** (d. 1956) stated that God created man with an inclination to accept what is true and beneficial and to be averse to what is false and harmful, this being the reality of the fiṭrah. He then stated, regarding the statement, "**Let there be no change in the creation of God**", "Meaning: No one is able to change the creation of God such that he can alter the created being into a form or mould other than the one which God has placed him in."[9]

Thus, no one is able to completely erase the fiṭrah which is deep and latent in every human being, even if it is concealed and buried to varying degrees through pride, arrogance and preference for lusts, desires, wealth and authority. This is why the staunchest and most arrogant of atheists such as Richard Dawkins can be found making the type of statement that was cited earlier.

---

[7] With respect to origin of life, it is impossible for life to arise *from non-life* purely through random physical and chemical interactions in the absence of **knowledge**, **choice**, **intent**, and **wisdom**. In other words, without some form of steering by an agent based on deep, vast, intricate knowledge.

[8] See: http://aboutatheism.net/?gsuaktr which discusses research at Oxford University by Justin Barrett and Olivera Petrovich.

[9] Refer to *Taysīr al-Karīm al-Raḥmān* (Cairo:Dār al-Ḥadīth) p. 703.

It should be noted from our discussion regarding the fiṭrah that all humans are equals at birth. This is evidence that Islām is the true religion because it is founded upon **universality** and **justice**. It is both a lie and injustice to claim that: a) there is a select group of chosen, favoured people who are above others merely because of their **lineage** or **caste**, or b) that humans are born **sinful** or with a burden of sin that they did not commit and can only be saved by **a blood-sacrifice**, or c) that humans are born **purposeless** and must therefore create their own subjective realities and purposes in life in order to be truly happy. These false foundations—*when turned into core elements of religious doctrine or used to generate lifestyle philosophies*—lead to racism, injustice and corruption because they are man-made constructs. These doctrines did not come from God, the Creator of all of humanity, and are not found in any revealed, uncorrupted book or on the tongue of any sent messenger, and nor do they have any sound, rational or empirical basis.

The **fiṭrah**—the *original disposition* which has been explained—and the **Messengers of God** who establish the truth through observed and rational evidences are the **two proofs** God will use against those who chose to reject His signs and preferred disbelief.[10] Likewise, against those who acknowledged Him and His favours yet erected false deities and worshipped them instead of or alongside Him. This is known as associationism (*shirk*) and is the greatest injustice because it is a violation of the universal order. This will be explained further in the chapters to follow.

---

[10] As for the ideologies of **philosophical naturalism** and **materialism** which underpin the atheistic frame of mind, these are nothing but sophisticated versions of nature worship in which the attributes of **knowledge**, **choice**, **intent**, **power** and **wisdom** are stripped from God (Allāh) and cryptically credited to nature through the use of highly technical language in **inventive theories** which are validated by maths rather than strict empirical means. There are only two possibilities. Either **choice with intent** is behind creation or it is **the pure randomness of physical and chemical interactions**. The study of the universe and its law-like organisation, and detailed investigation into the complexity of biological life bear witness to the otherwise obvious fact that there is **choice with intent** behind this creation.

Tawḥīd: The Core Of Islām

Based upon the above, the message and guidance of Islām appeals to and acts upon the fiṭrah. It nurtures this raw potential to inward and outward perfection through *beneficial knowledge* and *righteous action*. This guidance is based upon the fundamental facts and realities of human nature. **Therefore, Islām is but the attainment of peace and serenity in the heart and soul and outward nobility and perfection in character through sincere gratitude to God via righteous, beneficial works that have a rectifying influence upon the individual and the society.**

It is founded upon the firm conviction that no one deserves to be worshipped but God alone. **This is the ultimate truth upon which the universe stands and persists and to which it bears witness and from which the notion of justice emanates.** God alone is the creator of all elements, forces, entities, physical laws and cause-effect mechanisms through which living things arise and subsist and as such, He alone is worthy of worship. Muslims believe that this is the true basis for sound religion and that it is known innately, through intuition—without conscious reasoning—as well as through observation, reflection and reason via the physical senses and rational faculties.

Only God has the attributes of **independent creation, ownership and regulation** through a vast interconnected system of causes and effects—showing that He alone is the true giver and taker of life, absolute, independent controller of benefit and harm and sole owner of all the means of provision and subsistence. Therefore, it is only rational that He alone is thanked and worshipped for the innumerable favours which one enjoys on a daily basis.

God said in the Qurʾān:

يَا أَيُّهَا النَّاسُ اعْبُدُوا رَبَّكُمُ الَّذِي خَلَقَكُمْ وَالَّذِينَ مِن قَبْلِكُمْ لَعَلَّكُمْ تَتَّقُونَ الَّذِي
جَعَلَ لَكُمُ الْأَرْضَ فِرَاشًا وَالسَّمَاءَ بِنَاءً وَأَنزَلَ مِنَ السَّمَاءِ مَاءً فَأَخْرَجَ بِهِ مِنَ الثَّمَرَاتِ
رِزْقًا لَّكُمْ فَلَا تَجْعَلُوا لِلَّهِ أَندَادًا وَأَنتُمْ تَعْلَمُونَ

"O mankind, worship your Lord who created you and those before you so that you may be righteous. [He] who made for you the earth a repose [spread out] and the sky a ceiling and sent down

rain from the sky, and brought forth thereby fruits as provision for you. So do not set up rivals [in worship] to God (Allāh) while you know [that He alone is worthy of worship]." (2:21-22).

To single out God with all types and forms of worship and to shun the worship of all other deities which are assumed, invented and erected by men is the first and most important of Islam's five pillars. It is summarised in the statement:

لَا إِلَهَ إِلَّا اللهُ

There is no deity [worthy of being worshipped in truth]
but God [Allāh] alone [Lā ilāha ilallāh].

This is known as **Tawḥīd** (monotheism), or **the word (kalimah) of Islām.** It is the word of all the Messengers of God. It is that by which the heart attains true serenity, peace and satisfaction.

The entire Qur'ān is an elucidation of this statement. It presents proofs and signs for its truthfulness and for it being the greatest justice, from which all other manifestations of justice arise. It also presents arguments of reason to falsify what opposes it.

Upon this, God does not accept any act of devotion, or any act of goodness, benevolence and charity **unless it is founded upon firm conviction in the meaning of this statement**, which is: That none has the right to be worshipped but God alone and that only His worship is truth and justice and that worship of others besides or alongside Him is falsehood and injustice.

It is unjust and opposed to reason to invent, assume and erect deities from within God's creation, become attached to them and worship them, be they:

- celestial bodies, such as the earth, sun, moon and stars,
- trees, stones, statues and the likes,
- humans including the prophets and righteous living or dead,
- any other living creature or whatever has a life force,
- or any of the elements and forces.

These elements, entities and forces are created, subservient, themselves subject to laws **and do not independently control life, death, provision, sustenance, health, sickness, benefit or harm.** Thus, taking anything from them as deities alongside God, or as intermediaries that are invoked and worshipped in order to fulfil needs is baseless, opposes original disposition, common sense and reason and is the foundation of false religion.

Muslims hold that all of humanity was once united upon this way of worshipping God alone and that novel religions and schisms arose due to: a) exaggeration in the status of righteous people, b) awe of natural phenomena and of the life force in nature and c) awe of the celestial bodies and their movements. These affairs, coupled with ignorance, caused some among mankind to deviate from both natural inclination (fiṭrah) and sound reason (ʿaql) and led them to invent religions in which the worship of created elements, bodies, entities and forces was justified on **crude emotional grounds** or **reasoned philosophical ones.**[11]

God said in the Qurʾān:

كَانَ ٱلنَّاسُ أُمَّةً وَٰحِدَةً فَبَعَثَ ٱللَّهُ ٱلنَّبِيِّـۧنَ مُبَشِّرِينَ وَمُنذِرِينَ وَأَنزَلَ مَعَهُمُ ٱلْكِتَٰبَ بِٱلْحَقِّ لِيَحْكُمَ بَيْنَ ٱلنَّاسِ فِيمَا ٱخْتَلَفُوا۟ فِيهِ

"**Mankind was one nation [which was united upon Islām, but then became divided]. Then God (Allāh) sent the prophets as bringers of good tidings and warners and sent down with them the Scripture in truth to judge between the people concerning that in which they differed.**" (2:213).

Revelation came to guide them back to the truth and to resolve the differing they had fallen into regarding it.

This now leads us naturally to a discussion of the Prophets that were sent from time to time with a message from God to direct people back to their *natural inclination*, to that in which there is true serenity of the heart and soul, and peace of mind.

[11] Depature from the truth took place recurringly for the same basic reasons among nations across the Earth. When people saw the benefits and harms latent in natural phenomena such as the sun, rain, fire, rivers, animals, humans and so on, they began to assign divine attributes to these entities. They began to revere them—initially alongside God, and then later, besides God—so as to solicit benefits and ward off harms. This led to a decline in monotheistic belief and practice and the concurrent development of folk and cult religions in which those with an appetite for power, authority and wealth were able to manipuluate these aberrations of human instinct for their own personal, material benefit and also to gain power, authority and ascendancy. Such people became the first enemies to the Messengers of God.

Previous Prophets

Islām—which in its simplicity and universality has natural appeal to all people with intact **original disposition** and **uncorrupted reason**—was preached by all the Biblical Prophets: Noah, Abraham, Ishmael, Isaac, Jacob, Joseph, Moses, Aaron, Jesus and John (عَلَيْهِمُ السَّلَامُ). Muslims believe in and respect all of these prophets as an essential article of faith and are commanded by God with the following:

قُولُوا آمَنَّا بِاللَّهِ وَمَا أُنزِلَ إِلَيْنَا وَمَا أُنزِلَ إِلَىٰ إِبْرَاهِيمَ وَإِسْمَاعِيلَ وَإِسْحَاقَ وَيَعْقُوبَ وَالْأَسْبَاطِ وَمَا أُوتِيَ مُوسَىٰ وَعِيسَىٰ وَمَا أُوتِيَ النَّبِيُّونَ مِن رَّبِّهِمْ لَا نُفَرِّقُ بَيْنَ أَحَدٍ مِّنْهُمْ وَنَحْنُ لَهُ مُسْلِمُونَ

"Say, [O believers]: We have believed in God (Allāh) and what has been revealed to us and what has been revealed to Abraham and Ishmael and Isaac and Jacob and the Descendants [the Twelve Tribes] and what was given to Moses and Jesus and what was given to the Prophets from their Lord. We make no distinction between any of them, and we are Muslims [in submission] to Him." (2:136).

The previous prophets mentioned by name in the Qurʾān are:

1. Adam
2. Idrīs
3. Noah
4. Hūd
5. Ṣāliḥ
6. Lot
7. Abraham
8. Ishmael
9. Isaac
10. Jacob
11. Joseph
12. Shuʿayb
13. Aaron
14. Moses
15. David
16. Solomon
17. Job
18. Ezekiel
19. Jonah
20. Elias
21. Elisha
22. Zechariah
23. John
24. Jesus

There were many thousands of other prophets and every nation was sent a messenger at some point in its history.

The Torah, Psalms and Gospel *in their original forms* are also accepted by Muslims as revealed books. All of these books called to this same message. However, Muslims dispute the claim that these books remain in their original form today. This is due to irrefutable evidence—through both internal and external analysis—of the occurrence of loss, distortion, addition and alteration in the recording and transmission of these books. The Qurʾān, which is the spoken word of God, and its explainer Muḥammad (ﷺ) came to correct and confirm the truth that was in the original versions of past revealed books.

As such, Islām is not considered a new religion by Muslims but a confirmation and renewal of the religion of all previous Prophets.

God said about the people of past scripture:

وَمَا أُمِرُوا إِلَّا لِيَعْبُدُوا اللَّهَ مُخْلِصِينَ لَهُ الدِّينَ

“**They were not commanded except to worship God (Allāh) alone, making devotion purely and sincerely for Him alone**.” (98:5).

Traces of Islām’s greatest pillar—*pure monotheism in belief, speech and deed*—can still be found in the current forms of past revealed books. For example, in Deuteronomy 6:4 we find the word of Islām: «“Hear O Israel, the Lord our God, the Lord is one.”» And in Mark 12:29: «“‘The most important one,’ answered Jesus, ‘is this: ‘Hear, O Israel: The Lord our God, the Lord is one’.”»

The meaning is lost in translation, but these statements, in the original Hebrew or Aramaic (יְהוָה אֱלֹהֵינוּ, יְהוָה אֶחָד) and (יְהוָה אֶחָד וּשְׁמוֹ אֶחָד) would be identical to the statement **ilāhunā aḥād**—“Our Lord and Deity is uniquely one”—and in a verse of the Qurʾān (112:1): **qul huwallāhu aḥad**—“Say: He is Allāh [who is] Uniquely One”—and the declaration of monotheism in Islām, **lā ilāha illallāh,** which means: “None has the right to be worshipped but God (Allāh) alone.”

The learned scholars of the Children of Israel[12] knew full well that the message of the Qurʾān was the same as that of the books of their Prophets and that Islām was not a novel religion. They were reminded that before Muḥammad (ﷺ), **Jesus, the Son of Mary** (عَلَيْهِ ٱلسَّلَامُ) preached the same message to them after they had erred in doctrine, law and conduct. Since the vast majority of the Western world is Christian, the subject of Jesus in Islām requires a specific chapter.

---

[12] Cohenite priests descended from Aaron were present in Yathrib (Madīnah) during the era of the Prophet, and they were addressed by the Qurʾān.

Jesus (عَلَيْهِ السَّلَام) The Messiah

The position of Jesus (عَلَيْهِ السَّلَام) is a very lofty one in Islām. He was a prophet from a line of Prophets including Abraham, Moses, David and Solomon (عَلَيْهِمَا السَّلَام). The Qurʾān mentions how his birth was announced to Mary (عَلَيْهَا السَّلَام) who was favoured by God:

إِذْ قَالَتِ ٱلْمَلَٰٓئِكَةُ يَٰمَرْيَمُ إِنَّ ٱللَّهَ يُبَشِّرُكِ بِكَلِمَةٍ مِّنْهُ ٱسْمُهُ ٱلْمَسِيحُ عِيسَى ٱبْنُ مَرْيَمَ وَجِيهًا فِى ٱلدُّنْيَا وَٱلْءَاخِرَةِ وَمِنَ ٱلْمُقَرَّبِينَ.

"**[And mention] when the angels said, 'O Mary, indeed God (Allāh) gives you good tidings of a Word from Him, whose name will be the Messiah, Jesus, the son of Mary —distinguished in this world and the Hereafter and among those brought near [to God]'.**" (3:45).

Jesus (عَلَيْهِ السَّلَام) is the *Word of God* in the sense that He was created through God's word of command. He came to confirm the Torah (the law) and preach the Gospel (the news):

وَيُعَلِّمُهُ ٱلْكِتَٰبَ وَٱلْحِكْمَةَ وَٱلتَّوْرَىٰةَ وَٱلْإِنجِيلَ.

"**And He [God] will teach him the Book and the Wisdom and the Torah and the Gospel. And [make him] a messenger to the Children of Israel.**" (3:48).

The message of Jesus (عَلَيْهِ السَّلَام) was not new or unique: salvation through the worship of God alone. This entails pure monotheism in belief, speech and deed, and perfection of morals and character through observance of the law. As Jesus stated:

إِنَّ ٱللَّهَ رَبِّى وَرَبُّكُمْ فَٱعْبُدُوهُ هَٰذَا صِرَٰطٌ مُّسْتَقِيمٌ.

"**[Jesus]: Indeed, God (Allāh) is my Lord and your Lord, so worship Him alone. That is the straight path.**" (3:51).

Jesus (عَلَيْهِ السَّلَام) was given many signs to prove to the Children of Israel that he was indeed sent by God. A Muslim's faith is invalid without belief in Jesus. In light of the details presented below, Muslims are in fact the true followers of Jesus today, just as they are also the true followers of Moses and his message.[13]

---

[13] As for **Judaism**, this was not the name of the religion of Abraham, nor Isaac, nor Jacob, nor the Tribes, nor the early Israelites, nor Moses, nor David, nor Solomon (عَلَيْهِمَا السَّلَام). Judaism is named after the tribe of Judah, one of the twelve tribes of Israel. As a system, it did not develop until after the 6th century BC. The term "Judaism" was then applied *retrospectively* to encompass the period

Prophet Muḥammad (صَلَّى ٱللَّٰهُ عَلَيْهِ وَسَلَّمَ) said: "*Both in this world and the next, I am the nearest of all the people to the Son of Mary, and all the prophets are paternal brothers, and there has been no prophet between me and him (Jesus).*"[14] The Prophet also said: "*Whoever testifies that no deity is worthy of worship but God alone, without any partners, that Muḥammad is His servant and Messenger, that Jesus is the servant of God, His Word which He bestowed upon Mary, a Spirit from Him, and that Paradise is true and Hellfire is true, then he will enter Paradise through any of the eight gates of Paradise he wishes.*"[15]

Regarding the statement of God:

يَٰٓأَهْلَ ٱلْكِتَٰبِ لَا تَغْلُوا۟ فِى دِينِكُمْ وَلَا تَقُولُوا۟ عَلَى ٱللَّهِ إِلَّا ٱلْحَقَّ إِنَّمَا ٱلْمَسِيحُ عِيسَى
ٱبْنُ مَرْيَمَ رَسُولُ ٱللَّهِ وَكَلِمَتُهُۥٓ أَلْقَىٰهَآ إِلَىٰ مَرْيَمَ وَرُوحٌ مِّنْهُ فَـَٔامِنُوا۟ بِٱللَّهِ وَرُسُلِهِۦ وَلَا
تَقُولُوا۟ ثَلَٰثَةٌ ٱنتَهُوا۟ خَيْرًا لَّكُمْ إِنَّمَا ٱللَّهُ إِلَٰهٌ وَٰحِدٌ سُبْحَٰنَهُۥٓ أَن يَكُونَ لَهُۥ وَلَدٌ لَّهُۥ مَا فِى
ٱلسَّمَٰوَٰتِ وَمَا فِى ٱلْأَرْضِ وَكَفَىٰ بِٱللَّهِ وَكِيلًا.

"O People of the Scripture, do not commit excess in your religion and nor say about God (Allāh) except the truth. The Messiah, Jesus, the son of Mary, was but a messenger of God and His word which He directed to Mary and a soul [created at a command] from Him. So believe in God and His messengers. And

---

starting from the prophethood of Moses. *The name of true religion which God is pleased with for His creation is not tied to any race, tribe, gene or location. Hence, Hinduism, Buddhism, Judaism, Christianity and the likes are not names of the religion which God revealed to all of His prophets and messengers.* Further to the previous point, the *Jewish Encyclopedia* (1912) makes a distinction between the original Mosaic teachings and Rabbinic Judaism, a much later development which has remained the main form of Judaism until today. The Jewish Encylopedia also mentions that the original Israelite faith underwent frequent changes throughout the ages. It was strongly affected and moulded by the beliefs and practices of host nations such as Egypt, Persia and Babylonia. The Israelites also fell into wholesale apostacies throughout their history and also mingled among the nations. A Cohenite leadership—from the descendants of Aaron—was present in Madīnah during the Prophet's era. The Qur᾿ān reminded them and the Jews of the favours God had bestowed upon the Children of Israel when they were upon right guidance and were the best of nations in the earliest part of their history. It then described how the later ones departed from the guidance of Moses, fell into apostasy and polytheism, altered their scripture, distorted their law and contended with their prophets.

[14] Reported by Imām al-Bukhāri in his Ṣaḥīḥ.

[15] Reported by Imām Muslim in his Ṣaḥīḥ.

do not say, 'Three'. Desist, it is better for you. Indeed, God is but one deity. Exalted is He above having a son. To Him belongs whatever is in the heavens and whatever is on the earth. And sufficient is God as Disposer of affairs." (4:171).

This verse was revealed in relation to various factions of the Christians, such as the Jacobites, Nestorians and others. They had various sayings such as, "*Jesus is God*", others said, "*He is the Son of God*" and others said, "*He is the third of three.*"

The commentators of the Qurʾān provided the following general elaboration of the meaning of the above verse, as clarification and admonition for Christians:

O people of the Gospel, do not exceed the true belief and do not exaggerate and say of God except the truth. God has neither a son nor a wife. Jesus the Son of Mary was no more than a messenger like many other messengers before him. He was sent with the message of Islām which is to worship God alone, without ascribing any partners to Him. Jesus is the Word of God, with the meaning that he was created through a Word spoken by God which is "Be!" - not that he, Jesus, in his essence, is the actual Word of God. It was through this Word that Gabriel (*Jibrīl*) was sent and he breathed from the Spirit (*Rūḥ*) of God into Mary (عَلَيْهَاالسَّلَامُ). This Spirit is not a part of God's essence but a created entity which gave rise to life and its reality is unknown. The same Spirit was breathed into Ādam (عَلَيْهِالسَّلَامُ) who was born without father and mother. Through this Spirit came the miraculous birth of Jesus. **Hence, Jesus is the Word and the Spirit of God.** He was created through God's Word of command and the sending and breathing of the created Spirit through Gabriel. So people of the Gospel, believe in this truth regarding Jesus, the Son of Mary and submit to God alone. Shun the worship of all other deities and do not say "*There are three (deities),*" for there is only one deity worthy of worship in truth. You have unjustly raised Jesus from the station of servitude, prophethood and messengership to one of lordship (*rububiyyah*) and divinity (*ulūhiyyah*). Yet Jesus and his mother Mary were mere mortals, they ate, drank and walked the Earth and owned and controlled nothing in the heavens and Earth, save that God bestowed miracles upon Jesus as a sign of his prophethood. Desist from this statement of "Three," believe in the absolute oneness of God and worship only Him alone. This is the straight path indicated by authentic, uncorrupted revelation and sound reason.[16]

Traces of the original message of Jesus can be found in what is ascribed to Jesus in the current representations of the Gospel in the hands of the Christians.

In Mark 12:29 we find the word of Islām: «"The most important one," answered Jesus, "is this: 'Hear, O Israel: The Lord our God, the Lord is one'."» In John 17:3 we read: «"Now this is eternal life: that they know you, the only true God, and Jesus Christ, whom you have sent."» This is a reference to worshipping God alone and Jesus being sent as a prophet and messenger.

The believers in Jesus only knew him as a prophet. In Matthew 21:10-1 we read: «When Jesus had entered Jerusalem, the whole city was stirred and asked, "Who is this?" The crowds replied, "This is Jesus, the prophet from Nazareth in Galilee."» In Matthew 21:45-46 we read: «When the chief priests and the Pharisees heard Jesus's parables, they knew he was talking about them. They looked for a way to arrest him, but they were afraid of the crowd because the people held that he was a prophet.»

Jesus also made it clear that salvation and eternal life (in Paradise) is by observing the commandments.

In Matthew 19:16-17 there occurs: «Just then a man came up to Jesus and asked, "Teacher, what good thing must I do to get eternal life?" Jesus replied by saying: "If you want to enter life, keep the commandments."» In Matthew 5:17-20 we read: «"Do not think that I have come to abolish the Law or the Prophets; I have not come to abolish them but to fulfil them. For truly I tell you, until heaven and earth disappear, not the smallest letter, not the least stroke of a pen, will by any means disappear from the Law until everything is accomplished. Therefore anyone who sets aside one of the least of these commands and teaches others accordingly will be called least in the kingdom of heaven, but whoever practices and teaches these commands will be called great in the kingdom of

---

[16] Refer to the commentaries of Ibn Kathīr, al-Ṭabarī and al-Baghawi.

heaven. For I tell you that unless your righteousness surpasses that of the Pharisees and the teachers of the law, you will certainly not enter the kingdom of heaven."» Thus, to his followers, Jesus was no more than a prophet who called to pure monotheism, righteous works and observance of the law.

The Children of Israel split into two: **a)** those who believed in Jesus as Prophet and Messiah and **b)** those who rejected him out of anger and resentment for his criticism of their iniquities, excesses and departure from the law.

Those who believed in him also split into two:

- **Those who remained loyal to his teachings** from the Israelites, represented by James the Just. They are generally referred to as the early "Jewish Christians" by researchers.

- **Those who deviated from his teachings**. They are the Pauline Christians, led by Paul who had never met Jesus and was originally a persecuter of the followers of Jesus.

James Tabor, a professor of Religious Studies and a scholar of the origins of Christianity and ancient Judaism, writes: "**There are two completely separate and distinct Christianities embedded in the New Testament.** One is quite familiar and became the version of the Christian faith known to billions over the past two millennia. Its main proponent was the apostle Paul. The other has been largely forgotten and by the turn of the first century A.D. had been effectively marginalized and suppressed by the other... Its champion was no other than James..."[17]

As for Paul, he invented a mythological Jesus consistent with Greek and Roman pagan beliefs in human gods, sacrifices, saviours and redemptions bearing little to no resemblance to the historical Jesus as an Israelite prophet.[18]

---

[17] In *The Jesus Dynasty: The Hidden History of Jesus, His Royal Family and the Birth of Christianity*. New York: Simon and Schuster (2006). p. 261.

[18] "Paul's interpretation of the Christ figure bears the unmistakable stamp of a saviour figure of the Greek mystery religions into whose form Jesus was cast. The statements of Jesus Himself, however, do not support His exaltation to the Godhead... With the gradual demise of the Jewish wing of Christianity Paul's Christology came to the forefront in the Christian understanding on Jesus. His glorification of Christ's divinity has played a major role in the

Paul also removed righteous works from faith and abolished the necessity of law, thereby making it of no effect in salvation. He was considered an apostate from the law by Jesus's actual disciples and followers. His innovated religion spread through the aid of empire and with the formulation of the Trinity in the 5th century [on the back of Greek philosophical concepts][19] it became the dominant religion of the Western world. The connection to the actual beliefs and practices of Jesus the Israelite Prophet was lost by the time of the arrival of Prophet Muḥammad (صَلَّى ٱللَّهُ عَلَيْهِ وَسَلَّمَ).

Islām is a direct connection to the authentic teachings of Jesus (عَلَيْهِ ٱلسَّلَامُ) and to his immediate and direct followers such as James, and of the Israelite Prophets before him. Muslims believe in the Lord of Jesus, worship like Jesus, invoke God alone like Jesus, have the same dietary laws as Jesus and are circumcised just like Jesus. Devout Muslim women dress like Mary (عَلَيْهَا ٱلسَّلَامُ) and strive to mimic her piety, modesty and chastity. Both Jesus and Mary have a lofty position in the heart of every Muslim.

---

deification of Jesus." Jack Mclean in *The Deification of Jesus.* World Order, Spring Summer edition, 1980, p. 24.

[19] "Towards the end of the 1st century, and during the 2nd, many learned men came over both from Judaism and paganism to Christianity. These brought with them into the Christian schools of theology their Platonic ideas and phraseology." Mclintock, J. and Strong, J. in *Cyclopaedia of Biblical, Theological, and Ecclesiastical Literature*, 1891, Vol. 10, "Trinity," p. 553). "The use of Greek philosophy in Christian theology had far-reaching consequences for the core of Christology: the ontological terms *ousia*, *physis* and *prosopon* were introduced to explain and safeguard the mystery of Jesus Christ. In the process the Christian faith was dejudaized and Hellenized." Jongeneel, J. *Jesus Christ in World History.* (2009) p. 91. This explains why we see a transition in the status of Jesus in the early Gospel of Mark from being a prophet, a "son of man" who preaches worship of God alone, righteous works and adherence to the law as means of attaining the kingdom of God in the next life, to the status of Jesus in the later gospel of John as the "Son of God", then as the Word becoming flesh, God Incarnate and so on. This is clear evidence of the influence of Greek philosophy on the development of Christian theology. In Pauline Greco-Roman Christianity, Jesus was framed for Gentiles in a way very much like the gods they already knew and worshipped. Jesus was moved from an Israelite monotheistic setting to a pagan, polytheistic Greco-Roman setting. This very much suited evangelists trying to win converts.

On account of clear Qurāʾnic texts and Prophetic traditions, Muslims believe that righteous works are a vital part of faith.[20] They hold that salvation is through a combination of a) faith, works and observance of law on behalf of the servant as **necessary means** and b) grace, mercy and bounty on behalf of God as the **determining factor** in salvation and success. Each person is born clean and sinless, is responsible only for his or her own deeds and will not bear the burden of any other. This agrees perfectly with common sense and reason, is in perfect accord with divine justice, and was the original and actual teaching of the Gospel.

Muḥammad (ﷺ) was sent to revive this pristine way, the way of Abraham, Moses and Jesus (عَلَيْهِمُ السَّلَامُ).

For Jews and Christians who believe in Muḥammad (ﷺ) there is a double reward.

God (عَزَّوَجَلَّ) said:

ٱلَّذِينَ آتَيْنَاهُمُ ٱلْكِتَابَ مِن قَبْلِهِ هُم بِهِ يُؤْمِنُونَ. وَإِذَا يُتْلَىٰ عَلَيْهِمْ قَالُوٓاْ آمَنَّا بِهِ إِنَّهُ ٱلْحَقُّ مِن رَّبِّنَآ إِنَّا كُنَّا مِن قَبْلِهِ مُسْلِمِينَ. أُوْلَٰٓئِكَ يُؤْتَوْنَ أَجْرَهُم مَّرَّتَيْنِ بِمَا صَبَرُواْ

"Those to whom We gave the Scripture before it [the Qur'ān] they are believers in it. And when it is recited to them, they say: 'We have believed in it. Indeed, it is the truth from our Lord. Indeed [even] before it we were Muslims [submitting to God].' Those will be given their reward twice for their patience" (28.52-54).

This verse is a reference to the People of the Book who believed in their prophet—whether Moses or Jesus—and then believed in Muḥammad (ﷺ). For such Jews and Christians who accept Islām after having been faithful to whatever they possessed of the messages of Moses or Jesus there is a double reward for their patience and sincerity. This is indicated in the authentic traditions. Prophet Muḥammad (ﷺ) said: "*Three persons will receive a double reward*" and from them he mentioned, "*a man from the people of the Book who believes in his prophet and believes in Muhammad.*"[21]

---

[20] In his Epistle, James refutes the innovated doctrine of Paul that faith alone (devoid of works) justifies salvation. Refer to James 1:22-25 and James 2:14-26.

[21] Related by Imām al-Bukhārī.

Muḥammad (ﷺ) The Messenger

In light of what has preceded, the Prophet Muḥammad (ﷺ) did not come with a new religion.

God (Allāh) stated in the Qurʾān:

قُلْ مَا كُنتُ بِدْعًا مِّنَ الرُّسُلِ

"Say [O Muḥammad]: I am not a novel thing among the messengers." (46:9).

Rather, he only revived the religion of Abraham, Moses and Jesus (عَلَيْهِمُ ٱلسَّلَامُ) which was Islām. God (Allāh) said in the Qurʾān:

نَزَّلَ عَلَيْكَ الْكِتَابَ بِالْحَقِّ مُصَدِّقًا لِّمَا بَيْنَ يَدَيْهِ وَأَنزَلَ التَّوْرَاةَ وَالْإِنجِيلَ

"He has sent down upon you, [O Muḥammad], the Book in truth, confirming what [scripture] was before it. And He revealed the Torah and the Gospel." (3:3).

And also:

وَأَنزَلْنَا إِلَيْكَ الْكِتَابَ بِالْحَقِّ مُصَدِّقًا لِّمَا بَيْنَ يَدَيْهِ مِنَ الْكِتَابِ وَمُهَيْمِنًا عَلَيْهِ

"And We have revealed to you, [O Muḥammad], the Book in truth, confirming that which preceded it of the Scripture and as a criterion [of truth] over it." (5:48).

Prophet Muḥammad (ﷺ) was from the offspring of Ishmael (عَلَيْهِ ٱلسَّلَامُ), the son of Abraham (عَلَيْهِ ٱلسَّلَامُ). Abraham and Ishmael had settled in the western region of the Arabian peninsula known as the Hijāz and they built a house for God's worship in Mecca. This is the Kaʿbah in whose direction Muslims from all regions of Earth turn during their prayer to God. Abraham prayed for this city to be secure and for the region to be blessed with God's praise and His worship (Qurʾān 14:37)—a prayer whose fulfilment is evidently witnessed by the entire world today.

Muḥammad (ﷺ) was prophesied by the Israelite Prophets. His name, lineage and location were mentioned in the books in the hands of the Jews and in the Gospel of Jesus, he was mentioned as *Aḥmad*. This can still be traced in the current Gospels when the Greek is rendered back into the original Aramaic (Syriac) language, the language that Jesus actually spoke.

God (Allāh) said, referring to those Jews and Christians who recognised and believed in Muḥammad (ﷺ):

الَّذِينَ يَتَّبِعُونَ الرَّسُولَ النَّبِيَّ الْأُمِّيَّ الَّذِي يَجِدُونَهُ مَكْتُوبًا عِندَهُمْ فِي التَّوْرَاةِ وَالْإِنجِيلِ

"Those who follow the Messenger, the Unlettered Prophet, whom they find written in what they have of the Torah and the Gospel..." (7:157).

It is evident from the readings of the relevant texts in question[22] that a prophet named **Aḥmad** ("most praiseworthy") would appear among **an idol-worshipping nation** and whose message would be for all nations. He would be from the offspring of **Kedār, son of Ishmael**, and emerge from the deserts and mountains of **Paran** (Hijāz) in **a dry, arid, place** lacking vegetation (Mecca). He was described by the Prophet Isaiah as **Aḥmad**, as **God's servant** (ʿabd), **chosen one** (mukhtār) and **beloved** (ḥabīb) who would be received by people rejoicing at **the mountain of Selaʿ** (in Yathrib, Madīnah). His message would be directed towards his own idol-worshipping people who would fight him, though he would be victorious over them. He would also come with **a new hymn** (the Qurʾān) and **a new law**. He would be victorious over the nations and his praise and mention would become great.

These descriptions are highly specific and do not fit any Israelite Prophet. However, they match exactly, the descriptions of the Prophet of Islām in terms of his lineage, name, titles, location of appearance and settlement, the nature and content of his message, his adversaries, his victory, the spread of his call and the singing of his hymn, which is the Qurʾān, in all regions of the earth.

The Prophet (ﷺ) was sent at a time when the teachings and traces of past messengers in various parts of the world had been completely erased or distorted. The Pagans of Arabia had inherited

---

[22] Refer for example to Isaiah 42:1-25, 21:13-17, Habakkuk 3:3. It is important to study the texts of these prophecies through the original Hebrew—in the case of the Old Testament—and by rendering the Greek originals of the Gospels into Syriac (Aramaic)—the actual language spoken by Jesus. The languages of Hebrew, Arabic and Aramaic are very similar.

many of the deities of the ancients and worshipped them alongside God. The Sabeans worshipped the celestial bodies. The Jews and Christians had departed from the teachings of Moses and Jesus respectively. They had altered their religion through the distortion of their revealed books and the syncretisation of concepts and beliefs from other nations such as the Babylonians, Egyptians, Greeks, Persians and Romans. All other nations had likewise fallen into the worship of other deities besides or alongside God. Past messages of monotheism brought by messengers of God in various nations across the earth had long been lost or obscured through novel beliefs, concepts, rituals and practices.

From the start of his prophethood in 610 CE and for a period of 13 years in Mecca, the Prophet preached peacefully to the Pagan Arabs. He invited them to single out God (Allāh) in worship and shun the worship of deities that have no power over benefit or harm. He spoke against their racism, their maltreatment of women and slaves, killing of female newborns, disdain of the poor, weak and needy and other misdeeds. He enjoined benevolence to widows and orphans and the frequent giving of charity.

Unfortunately, his message was not in the personal, economic and political interests of the pagans of Mecca.

He was shown hostility and his believing companions were oppressed, tortured and murdered. Attempts were made on his life and he was forced to migrate to what became known as the city of Madīnah in 622 CE. He continued preaching for another ten years whilst facing hostility, plots and the machinations of the polytheists and various forces who formed alliances and initiated wars against him.

Being granted permission to ward off aggression and injustice from himself and his believing companions, he only fought to defend the instrument of peaceful preaching so that the message of Islām, genuine monotheism and perfection of morals and character, could be heard by others without hindrance.

After inviting the Pagan Arabs, he also invited the Jews back to the original, uncorrupted religion of Prophet Moses (عَلَيْهِ السَّلَامُ). Through the Qurʾān, he reminded them of how the Children of

Israel were favoured when they adhered to right guidance and how their leaders strayed, fell into disbelief, opposed the Prophets, distorted the Book, altered the law, entered into magic and other iniquities. He also argued with the Christians and invited them to the true religion of Prophet Jesus (عَلَيْهِ السَّلَامُ). He explained the falsehood of the Trinity, that Jesus was not divine, never claimed to be and never asked to be worshipped. He explained through the argument of the Qurʾān that Jesus called to the worship of the one true deity, God (Allāh), and none other, and that his mother was but a chaste, truthful, righteous woman, chosen by God over all other women.

Despite many wars waged to extinguish his message, the Prophet came out victorious. The entire Arabian peninsula entered Islām during the last two years of his prophethood, willingly and without compulsion, when they saw his victory over Quraysh and it allies, coupled with their firm belief that God would never give custody of Mecca to an imposter and liar. His followers were victorious over the great nations of the time, the Romans and Persians. Over the passing of centuries, Islām eventually spread all the way to westernmost Africa, reached France and Switzerland on one side of the Earth and northern Australia on the other side.[23]

Islām—in its beliefs, teachings and codes—takes humans from their innate predisposition towards good to the peak of perfection in human character and morals. At the same time, it protects them from that in which lies the destruction of individuals, societies and nations. In the following two chapters we will look at how this is achieved through Islām's **greatest pillars and obligations** and its **greatest prohibitions**.

---

[23] Unlike Christian European colonialism, the spread of Islām was not accompanied by the wholesale slaughter and organised extermination of indigenous people. For a scholarly and objective, non-Muslim's treatment of the spread of Islām, refer to the book, "*The Preaching of Islam*", by the British Orientalist scholar and historian, Thomas Walker Arnold (d. 1930), London Constable & Company, 1913.

Pillars and Obligations

The first pillar of Islām is pure monotheism and affirmation of the messengership of Muḥammad (ﷺ) which incorporates belief in all previous prophets and messengers as has preceded. There are another four pillars which in addition to the first comprise the essence of Islām as outwardly observed:

Daily prayers in a state of physical cleanliness as a form of devotion and gratitude to God for his innumerable favours is the second greatest pillar. The prayer provides a daily, direct and constant connection with God upon which all moral conduct is hinged. When performed sincerely and correctly, it prevents from shameful and evil deeds (Qurʾān 29:45). When insincere and done for show, it will have little to no effect.

Fasting the month of Ramaḍān as a means of exercising patience and developing sympathy for the hungry and needy is a bodily act of worship and the next greatest pillar. Through it, a Muslim is reminded that all food and drink comes through a vast system of interconnected causes and effects created and controlled by God. Being without food and drink from dawn to sunset is a reminder of this fact and develops humility, gratefulness and piety.

Giving obligatory charity to the poor and needy to the equivalent of 2.5% of any excess wealth unused for one lunar year having a value greater than 85 grams of gold. This reminds a Muslim that wealth—created by God and which facilitates the attainment of worldly needs and interests—belongs ultimately to God. As such, we are only temporary custodians of it and must dispose of it in accordance with His good pleasure, for the beneficial interests of others. Hence, voluntary charity is also highly emphasised.

Performing pilgrimage (hajj) to Mecca when one has the means to do so is an enactment of the actions of Prophet Abraham who built the House of God's worship in Mecca with his son Ishmael. Every nation has rituals but the rituals of hajj symbolise strict, pure monotheism completely free of all traces of polytheism, idolatry and the worship of others besides God. People from every corner of the Earth come in a white garment and are indistinguishable in terms of class or wealth. They are equal before their Lord and Creator whether they are blue, brown, grey or green-eyed or white, brown, black or red-skinned.

So these are the five pillars of Islām. One can see what they contain of tremendous cultivation of the soul and preparing it to become a repository for every type of goodness. The qualities of humility, gratitude, patience, compassion and sacrifice developed through these pillars of Islām are the fabric upon which **moral conduct** and **perfection of human character** are built.

Thereafter, **honouring one's parents, relatives, neighbours and guests**—*whether Muslim or non-Muslim*—are among the most emphatic of deeds in Islam after the five pillars.

As for **honouring the parents**, then sufficient an illustration is the fact that a Muslim is commanded to maintain kindness and keep beautiful company with parents **even if they are polytheists who strive to make him or her worship other deities besides God**. To associate partners with God in worship is the most heinous deed and the only unforgiveable sin in Islām, if a person dies upon it.

God said:

وَوَصَّيْنَا الْإِنسَانَ بِوَالِدَيْهِ حَمَلَتْهُ أُمُّهُ وَهْنًا عَلَىٰ وَهْنٍ وَفِصَالُهُ فِي عَامَيْنِ أَنِ اشْكُرْ لِي وَلِوَالِدَيْكَ إِلَيَّ الْمَصِيرُ وَإِن جَاهَدَاكَ عَلَىٰ أَن تُشْرِكَ بِي مَا لَيْسَ لَكَ بِهِ عِلْمٌ فَلَا تُطِعْهُمَا وَصَاحِبْهُمَا فِي الدُّنْيَا مَعْرُوفًا ۖ وَاتَّبِعْ سَبِيلَ مَنْ أَنَابَ إِلَيَّ ثُمَّ إِلَيَّ مَرْجِعُكُمْ فَأُنَبِّئُكُم بِمَا كُنتُمْ تَعْمَلُونَ

"And We have enjoined upon man [care] for his parents. His mother carried him, [increasing her] in weakness upon weakness, and his weaning is in two years. Be grateful to Me and to your parents; to Me is the [final] destination. But if they endeavor to make you associate with Me that of which you have no knowledge, do not obey them but accompany them in [this] world with

kindness and follow the way of those who turn back to Me [in repentance]." (31:14-15).

The scholar and Qurʾānic commentator al-Baghawī (d. 1122) said: "It means benevolence, keeping ties with them and beautiful companionship."[24]

Of the parents, the mother has the greatest right and is most deserving of kindness and benevolence. A man came to the Prophet (ﷺ) and asked: "Who has the greatest right to my kind companionship?" The Prophet said: "*Your mother.*" The man asked: "Then who?" He said: "*Your mother.*" The man asked: "Then who?" He again said: "*Your mother.*" The man asked: "Then who?" Then the Prophet said: "*Your father.*"[25]

As for **honouring the neighbor**, it is the greatest of rights after the rights of parents and blood-relatives and applies to every neighbour. The Prophet (ﷺ) was commanded to emphatically stress this right. He said, "*The [angel] Gabriel has not ceased advising me with respect to the neighbour until I thought he (the neighbour) would be made to inherit (from his fellow neighbour).*"[26] The Prophet also negated complete faith from the one who does not withhold from harming his neighbour, "*By God, he does not have faith, by God, he does not have faith, by God, he does not have faith whose neighbour is not safe from his harm.*"[27] And in another authentic tradition, he said, "*Whoever believes in God and the Final Day (of Reckoning), let him honour his neighbour.*"[28] Under the chapter heading, "The Jewish Neighbour," the famous collector of Prophetic traditions, Imām al-Bukhārī relates the following authentic tradition from the famous commentator of the Qurʾān, Mujāhid (d. 722), who said: "I was with ʿAbd Allāh bin ʿAmr whilst his servant was preparing a sheep [for a meal] and he said, 'O servant! When you have finished [cooking the meal] then begin by offering to our Jewish neighbour [first].' So a man present said, "The Jew, may God rectify you?' He replied, 'I

[24] Maʿālim al-Tanzīl (6/288).
[25] Related by al-Bukhārī (no. 5626).
[26] Reported by Muslim in his Ṣaḥīḥ.
[27] Related by al-Bukhārī in Kitāb al-Adab.
[28] Related by al-Bukhārī and Muslim.

heard the Prophet (ﷺ) advising with [kindness] to the neighbour [with such emphasis] until we feared he would relate to us [through revelation] that the [neighbour] is to inherit [from his fellow neighbour]'."[29]

The neighbour in Islām is defined as the one who lives in the vicinity of any direction, left, right, front, back and would also include above and below in flats and apartments.

As for **honouring the guest**, whether Muslim and non-Muslim, the Prophet (ﷺ) said: "*Whoever believes in God and the Last Day, let him honour the guest.*"[30] The famous scholar of Prophetic traditions Imam al-Nawawī (d. 1277) stated: "The Muslims are united upon honouring the guest and that it is from the most emphasised deeds of Islām."[31]

There are many qualities and other deeds of virtue which Islām enjoins and which are too numerous to mention. Through the emphasised and regular obligations, as well as the commended actions, Muslims are encouraged to achieve excellence (iḥsān) in their piety and devotion, this being the highest of ranks within Islām.

It should be noted that a righteous deed is only a righteous deed if it is founded upon pure monotheism, *Tawḥīd*. If deeds are hinged upon beliefs which violate this central teaching of the Prophets and Messengers, they are not accepted by God. This means that righteous deeds performed by polytheists, idolators and those who worship others alongside God are in vain. This is because inventing deities, ascribing divine attributes to them and soliciting them for good and repelling or lifting harm—despite them being no more than subservient creatures of God with **no independent power** over the affairs sought from them—comprise the greatest injustice. These deeds comprise gross rejection of the universal order as well as revilement of the intellect.

---

[29] Related by al-Bukhārī in *al-Adab al-Mufrad*.
[30] Related by al-Bukhārī and Muslim.
[31] Sharḥ al-Nawawī ʿalā Muslim (3/393).

The Major Prohibitions

The major prohibitions in Islam—after polytheism, idolatry and other forms of associationism (shirk)— include:

- **murder**,
- **usury (interest)**,
- **adultery and fornication**,
- **alcohol**,
- **gambling**,
- **cutting off from one's parents** and
- **giving false witness** and numerous others.

These crimes and vices lead to loss of life and harm to health, wealth and personal dignity and corruption of society. Any benefit in these vices is negligible and restricted.

These affairs cause harm and decay to society over time despite the financial benefit gained by a small minority of evil people who profit immensely by commercialising these vices or despite the temporal pleasures gained by those who indulge in them, whether occasionally or habitually.

Some of these vices become punishments upon minds, bodies, families and societies when they turn into addiction. Hence, these vices are seen as **nation destroyers**.

It grieves Muslims to see the societies they live in suffer from the harms inevitably produced by these vices, including the loss of life, broken homes, abuse, sickness, wastage and so on.

Usually, the greatest opponents and enemies of Islām and of the teachings of the Prophets of God in general **are those with vested interests**. They stand to lose most if people give up enslavement to false deities, exploitative lifestyle philosophies, desires of the soul, vices and harmful practices—and instead, submit to God alone. By adhering to His commands and prohibitions they are freed from the clutches of exploiters and profiteers and attain true freedom from enslavement.

As for these vices, these nation destroyers, over long periods of time—in a slow, imperceptible manner—they lead to:

a) loss or confiscation of **private property**[32] from individuals and economic enslavement of nations and their subjects in the case of **usury** as well as the usurpation of political power from nation states[33] by those who issue currency as a usurious debt instrument.

b) harm to wealth, health, intellect, family and children in the case of **alcohol**,[34] and **gambling.**[35]

---

[32] **Private property** forms the basis of many other rights and its destruction is the destruction of individual freedom. Islām is vehemently against the confiscation of private property through its condemnation of and severe prohibition against oppressive economic and trade practices, chief of which is usury. For this reason, devout Muslims and Muslim rulers—in obedience to God—do not partake in usury or interest-based banking practices in order to protect the economic interests of the nation and its political power from being usurped. By shunning interest, devout Muslims are indirectly aiding the citizens of whichever nation they reside in. This is because they take no part in increasing the communal burden known as the "national debt" which is forced upon the entire nation through a usurious, debt-based economy.

[33] **Usurious central banks** are the instruments of this process. Since political power always follows economic power as a fundamental law of human activity, then the usurpation and control of economic power in this manner leads to the hijacking of nations and their political independence. As such, nations can be coerced into actions (such as **invasions**, **wars** or **implementing policies for the benefit of private banks and corporations**) which are not in the interests of their economies nor their citizens. As a result, institutions, processes and mechanisms that are supposed—*or alleged*—to work for the citizens (such as *government, democracy*) become meaningless, empty slogans and of no effect. Today, the majority of developed western nations are run as *socialist democracies*, which—ignoring the illusory layer of token democracy—are stealth, subtle and graduated implementations of most of the planks of Karl Marx's *Communist Manifesto*. These include *heavy progressive taxation, centralisation of all credit, abolition of private property and inheritance rights, centralised control of the means of communication and transport, equal liability to labour* (a social welfare scheme) and *free education to prepare children to work* for the communal debt-slave system by combining education with industrial production.

[34] **Alcohol** negatively impacts the brain, heart, liver, pancreas and the immune system. The many diseases produced as a result (including a range of cancers) lead to tremendous financial burdens upon the economies of nations. On average, around **50% of all violent crime** is committed under the influence of alcohol. Statistics also indicate a similar link between alcohol consumption, domestic violence and sexual assault. A 2012 document titled

c) breakdown of the family institution and thereby lineage and thereby the gradual loss of inheritance and property rights[36] in the

---

"The Government's Alcohol Strategy" by the UK Secretary of State for the Home Office declares: "Society is paying the costs – alcohol-related harm is now estimated to cost society £21 billion annually." In August 2018, Lancet, the science journal, published a huge global study establishing that there is no safe limit in the consumption of alcohol. The report concludes: "Alcohol use is a leading risk factor for disease burden worldwide, accounting for nearly 10% of global deaths among populations aged 15–49 years, and poses dire ramifications for future population health in the absence of policy action today. The widely held view of the health benefits of alcohol needs revising, particularly as improved methods and analyses continue to show how much alcohol use contributes to global death and disability. Our results show that the safest level of drinking is none. This level is in conflict with most health guidelines, which espouse health benefits associated with consuming up to two drinks per day. Alcohol use contributes to health loss from many causes and exacts its toll across the lifespan, particularly among men." Refer to "*Alcohol use and burden for 195 countries and territories, 1990–2016: a systematic analysis for the Global Burden of Disease Study 2016*" in Lancet 2018; 392: 1015–35. **This study proves that there is zero net benefit in alcohol**. By shunning alcohol, devout Muslims save the lives of people and protect their own health and that of others. They relieve the health services and thereby lift economic burdens, something for which they should be thanked.

[35] The **effects of gambling** are well-researched in the scientific literature. It creates impaired family relationships, emotional problems and financial difficulties. Evidence clearly and consistently establishes a link between gambling problems and family (domestic) violence. Children of gambling parents are also at a much higher risk of developing the same problem compared to others. Also, gambling leads to crime, bankruptcies and family breakdown. A report reveals the staggering cost of gambling: "The extent of Britain's addiction to controversial casino-style gambling machines is revealed today with the disclosure by two bookmaker giants that more than £12 billion was wagered on their machines in the first half of this year." Refer to "*Revealed: The £46bn cost of Britain's roulette machine addiction*". Daily Mail 5 August 2012. Non-Muslim governments allow gambling practices—stealth forms of organised looting of the masses already suffering from economic hardships—and then try to manage the consequences at tremendous cost to society. Islāmic law eliminates the problem from its very roots.

[36] Blood and family relations form the basis of **inheritance and property rights** through which property and wealth remain in private hands, allowing varying degrees of economic independence to private individuals. The promotion of sexual permissiveness and so-called *sexual liberation* is simply a means of eroding the family institution, which in turn leads to the erosion of private property and inheritance rights. When sex is promoted outside of the

case of **sexual promiscuity** and **sexual liberation lifestyle philosophies**, as well as the emergence and spread of diseases that harm and place burdens upon society in numerous ways.[37]

---

institution of marriage and outside of the union of a biological male and biological female, it leads to the gradual erosion of property and inheritance rights because the basis of the transfer of property and wealth between private individuals is the family and ties of blood. Homosexuality, lesbianism, gender confusion, transgenderism and early sexualisation of children all undermine the family institution and erode the underlying basis for these rights. These lifestyles are promoted predominantly by Marxists, Socialists, Communists and Collectivists who are the enemies of private property and who see in sexual liberation philosphies a powerful tool for the attainment of ideological, social and economic objectives.

[37] Sexual promiscuity leads, naturally, to **the spread of disease** in societies. Many reports on the subject over the past couple of decade indicate the following realities:

- The soaring of sexually transmitted diseases (STDs) coincides with a culture of promiscuity,
- In Britain and the US, Chlamydia, gonorrhoea and syphilis continue to grow despite sex education programs, promotion of "safer sex" and use of contraceptives,
- Abortion rates naturally increase with unwanted pregnancies,
- It is young people that are disproportionately affected,
- Casual sex increases mental health problems and depression.

See *Record rise in sexual diseases among promiscuous young adults*. Daily Mail, Jul. 16, 2008. ; *CDC: 'Alarming' increase in STDs*. USA Today, Nov. 18, 2015; CDC: *Sexually transmitted disease rates are rising*. USA Today, Oct. 19, 2016; *Study: Casual teen sex linked to higher depression rates*. Cornell Chronicle (Cornell University) Dec. 4, 2012.

◉ Sexual promiscuity is like gambling and alcohol in the sense that non-Muslim nations allow these vices to take place believing that regulation and education will limit their harms to society. This allows populations to be exploited by business interests who—through detailed long-term population studies—understand the human instinct, motivation and psychology to a level that enables them to engineer maximum exploitation. With this knowledge, they commercialise vices in order to profit immensely. However, society has to bear the burden of all the costs associated with the negative effects brought about through these vices, which are always inevitable.

In Islām, the solution is simple because **it cuts off everything at its roots**: Usury, alcohol and gambling are completely unlawful and sexual relations and intimacy are kept within the context of deep, meaningful, long-term, faithful relationships with chaste partners. This leads to the creation of mentally and psychologically sound offspring and strong, stable societies.

Hence, the prohibition of these vices in Islam whose laws are aimed at protecting: **life** (nafs), **property, wealth** (māl), **intellect** (ʿaql) and **lineage, honour** (nasl, ʿirḍ) through ways that are simple and effective and also aligned with the fundamental facts and realities of human nature. Islām does not allow business models to be built on top of vices and harmful practices in which a few profit at the expense of millions of others, even if some pleasure or gain is acquired by those millions in the process.

Those who are most opposed and hostile to Islām are those with vested interests in the perpetuation of these vices. Likewise, those who prefer vices, or attainment of fame or power over gratitude to God (Allāh)—through whose creative power such people enjoy the pleasures of the world on a daily basis. Much of the propaganda against Islām and Muslims can be put into context from this perspective, in addition to the fact that the most strategic and resource-rich locations in the world are populated by Muslims. Thus, invasions and wars are justified by presenting these populations as ignorant, backward and inherently violent due to their adherence to Islām. In reality, Islām has everything that can save exploited and ailing Western societies from their social and moral decadence, their economic woes, and their eventual ruin.

Incidentally, the largest group of converts to Islām—*despite the tremendous amount of anti-Islām propaganda*—are educated Christian women from Western nations who spend many years studying Islām before converting.[38] They convert for two main reasons. The

---

Islām rectifies societies and saves them from destruction. It saves them from exploitation and from becoming slaves to their desires.

[38] News headlines over the past twenty years abound in this regard: "*Why are so Many Modern British Career Women Converting to Islām*", Daily Mail, 28 October 2010. "*Europeans Increasingly Converting to Islam*", Gatestone Institute, 27 January 2012. "*Surge in Britons converting to Islam: White women lead a wave of Britons embracing Islam*" The Telegraph, 4 January 2011. "*How 100,000 Britons Have Chosen To Become Muslim... And Average Convert Is 27-Year-Old White Woman*", Daily Mail, 5 January 2011. "*Converts to Islām increase after French attack*", World Bulletin, 24 February 2015. "*More in France are Turning to Islām, Challenging a Nation's Idea of Itself*", NY Times, 3 February 2013. "*Islām is Ireland's Fastest Growing Religion*", International Business Times, 21 February 2014. This article points out that most of the converts are women. "*Lifting the*

first is a clear, lucid explanation of divinity in Islām, devoid of mystery, confusion and bewilderment. The second is that they see within Islām a coherent, practical framework of moral and social guidance which they found missing in their former lives leaving them empty and disillusioned despite having material comforts, apparent happiness and successful careers.

In a 2010 survey, conducted by Kevin Brice from Swansea University in Wales, converts to Islām identified "*alcohol and drunkenness*," a "*lack of morality and sexual permissiveness*" and "*unrestrained consumerism*" as negative aspects of British culture. The survey also revealed that nearly two thirds of the converts were women, more than 70% were white and the average age at conversion was just 27.[39] In short, intellectual and spiritual fulfilment coupled with moral direction and inner serenity are the main factors in their conversion to Islām.

☙

The **divorcing of works from faith** and the **abolition of the necessity of law for salvation** in Pauline Christianity set up Christian nations to become brittle, hollow and non-resilient, the effects of which are clearly visible in these nations today. When the age of empire came to an end for Christianity, and Christian nations entered the era of secularism, materialistic and liberal philosophies and various social, political and economic doctrines devised to erode and destroy the concept of national sovereignty, it was brought to its knees.

The people of these nations, their traditional values, and their overall wealth, health and independence have been harmed by private international banks that hijack and manipulate economies through usurious debt-based credit creation, alcohol consumption,

---

Veil on Ireland's Fastest Growing Religion", Independent Ireland, 21 September 2014. "*Islām Growing in America*", US Department of Defence, 4 October 2001. "*Hispanic Islāmic Converts Find Comfort in God and Latino Culture*", Huffington Post, 11 September 2012.

[39] Refer to *A Minority Within a Minority: A Report on Converts to Islam in the United Kingdom*, Kevin Brice (2010).

gambling, sexual promiscuity, the marketing of homosexuality and lesbianism as desirable lifestyles, the orchestrated promotion of gender confusion, early sexualisation of children, emasculation of men and the erosion of the family and traditional values.

There are movements in Western nations of white Christian backgrounds which have recognised these realities and are trying to address the harms. Often—due to the geopolitics of today—and due to uncritical acceptance of media narratives, they are inclined towards blaming Islām, and thereby Muslims, and see in a stricter return to Christianity, a solution.

However, an innovated religion in which ⇨

- Jesus has been made divine like Greco-Roman gods,
- Idols and statues are worshipped,
- The scripture is distorted and has lost integrity,
- The law is abolished and
- Salvation is justified by belief alone, without works,

⇨ will never be able to offer protection to the individual or the society and nor will it be able to ward off subversive doctrines and lifestyle philosophies. A religion in which salvation is through a doctrine of blood-sacrifice devoid of law does not have the capacity to rectify the servant or the land.

If these movements want to follow authentic religion, protect their morality and find salvation through **the way that Jesus actually practised and preached**—as opposed to what Greek evangelists writing in the second century CE falsely attributed to him in order to win converts from the pagan audiences of Greece and Rome—then they will find it only in Islām which is the call of all of the Messengers of God.[40] Thus, we advise these concerned movements—***whom we empathise with***—to shake off the centuries-old bias and look at Islām with new, clean spectacles.

After the **greatest obligations** and **greatest prohibitions** of Islām are the subjects of ethics, just dealings and perfection in character. The legislation of Islām draws out and cultivates these qualities in its adherents with the aim of perfecting character.

---

[40] Refer to *Jesus in Islām, Christianity and the Jewish Talmūd* (2017) by the author and to the website http://www.islamjesus.ws for more information.

Justice, Kind Dealings and Ethics

Muslims are obligated to speak good to people, behave justly and ethically, fulfil their contracts and abide by all of their agreements. God said in the Qur'ān:

وَقُولُوا لِلنَّاسِ حُسْنًا

"**And speak good with people...**" (2:83).

The contemporary Muslim scholar, **Shaykh Ṣāliḥ Āl al-Shaykh**, said in relation to this verse: "Justice is the foundation for all mutual interactions with non-Muslims, likewise, being kind to them, likewise speaking good to them. All of this is with respect to those who do not display enmity to Islām and its adherents."[41]

That justice is the primary foundation for all dealings with all people, irrespective of creed or race, is clear from another verse of the Qur'ān:

لَّا يَنْهَاكُمُ اللَّهُ عَنِ الَّذِينَ لَمْ يُقَاتِلُوكُمْ فِي الدِّينِ وَلَمْ يُخْرِجُوكُم مِّن دِيَارِكُمْ أَن تَبَرُّوهُمْ وَتُقْسِطُوا إِلَيْهِمْ إِنَّ اللَّهَ يُحِبُّ الْمُقْسِطِينَ

"**God (Allāh) does not forbid you from being kind and acting justly towards those who did not fight you because of religion and did not expel you from your homes. Indeed, God loves those who act justly.**" (60:8).

The famous Muslim Qur'ān commentator, **Ibn Jarīr al-Ṭabarī** (d. 932) said regarding this verse:

"The most correct of these statements is of the one who said that [this verse] pertains to all of the factions from the varying beliefs and religions. That you behave kindly towards them, and that you are just regarding them, because God (Allāh) generalised with His saying, '**...those who fought not against you on account of your religion and did not drive you out of your homes.**' So this applies to everyone who is characterised by this. He did not specify some as opposed to others in this regard."[42]

---

[41] *Hādhā Huwa al-Islām* (p. 18), from a transcribed lecture given in front of an audience of people of knowledge and influence.

[42] Refer *to Jāmiʿ al-Bayān* of Ibn Jarīr al-Ṭabarī under this particular verse.

In the context of this same verse, the Muslim jurist **Aḥmad bin Idrīs al-Miṣrī** (d. 1285) stated regarding interaction between Muslims and non-Muslims:

"The covenant of the guarantee of safety (**dhimmāh**)[43] obligates certain rights from us which are due to them—[the non-Muslims]—because they are in our neighbourhood and under our protection. They are under the protection (dhimmah) of God the Most High, of the Prophet (صَلَّى ٱللَّهُ عَلَيْهِ وَسَلَّمَ) and of Islām. Whoever transgressed against them even if it was with an evil word or backbiting them with respect to the honour of one of them, or any harm among the types of harm—or who even aided in that—then he has ruined the guarantee of (safety) of God, of His Messenger (صَلَّى ٱللَّهُ عَلَيْهِ وَسَلَّمَ) and of the religion of Islām that had been granted to them..."

And then he explained the meaning of being kind as mentioned in the verse mentioned earlier:

"To show gentleness to their weak, to satisfy the needs of their poor, to feed their hungry, to clothe their naked, to use gentle, kind speech to them from the angle of compassion and mercy towards them—not out of fear or inferiority—to bear whatever harm arises from them when they are our neighbours despite having the ability to end (their harm), doing this out of compassion for them, not out of fear or veneration of them. To supplicate for guidance for them, that they be made people of happiness, to advise them in all their affairs that pertain to their religion and [likewise] their worldly affairs. To protect them in their absence when anyone embarks upon harming them, to protect their wealth, their families, their honour and all of their rights and

---

[43] The dictionary meaning of *dhimmah* is: covenant, contract, bond, protection, shelter, alliance, responsibility, clientship, care, custody, coventant of protection, inviolability, security of life and property, the neglect of which brings blame. In his famous Arabic Lexicon, Edward Lane summarises the essence of the meaning of *dhimmah* as: "A sacred thing which one is under an obligation to reverence, respect, or honour, and defend; everything entitled to reverence, respect, honour or defence in the character and appertenances of a person; security, safety, security of life and property protection or safeguard; a promise, or an assurance, of safety, protection, or safeguard, indemnity." Refer to Lane's Lexicon, and also the dictionaries of Steingass and Hans Wehr.

beneficial interests. That they are supported in repelling any oppression against them and delivering all their rights to them. A (Muslim) does all such acts of goodness towards them that one who is in a privileged position can possibly do towards the one who is under-privileged and likewise, [all acts of goodness] that [even] an enemy could possibly do towards an enemy, for all of that is from nobility in character and manners. It is desireable that all of what we do with respect to them is from this angle, not from the angle of pride and loftiness on our behalf and nor from the angle of belittling ourselves and exalting them through such actions towards them."[44]

Treachery, dishonesty and injustice are severely prohibited by Islām and are traits of hypocrisy which clash with faith. The Quran orders: "**And fulfil every covenant, for every covenant will be enquired into.**" (17:35). The Prophet Muhammad (صَلَّىٰ ٱللَّٰهُ عَلَيْهِ وَسَلَّمَ) said: "*There are four traits, whoever possesses them is a hypocrite and whoever possesses some of them has an element of hypocrisy until he leaves it: The one who when he speaks he lies, when he promises he breaks his promise, when he disputes he transgresses, and when he makes an agreement he violates it.*"[45] These behaviours cannot be reconciled with faith and are antithetical to them.

The late and famous Salafi scholar of Saudi Arabia **Muḥammad bin Ṣāliḥ al-'Uthaymīn** (d. 2001) advised a gathering of over two-thousand Muslims in the city of Birmingham, United Kingdom, via tele-link on 28 July 2000 with the following words:

"I invite you to have respect for the [non-Muslims] who have the right that they should be respected, those with whom there is an agreement [of protection] for you. For the land in which you are living is such that there is an agreement between you and them... So preserve this agreement, and do not prove treacherous to it, since treachery is a sign of the hypocrites, and it is not from the way of the believers. Do not be fooled by the sayings of those

---

[44] Refer to his work *al-Furūq* (3/14). He is known as al-Qarāfī, and is a famous Mālikī jurist.

[45] Related by al-Bukhārī and Muslim.

foolish people[46], those who say 'These people are non-Muslims, so their wealth is lawful for us [to misappropriate or take by way of murder and killing].' For by God, this is a lie. A lie about God's religion, and a lie about Islāmic societies. We cannot say that it is lawful to be treacherous towards people whom we have an agreement with. O my brothers, O youth, O Muslims, be truthful in your buying and selling, and renting, and leasing, and in all mutual transactions. Because truthfulness is from the characteristics of the believers, and God, Blessed and Exalted, has commanded truthfulness in His saying, **'O you who believe, fear and keep your duty to God (Allāh) and be with the truthful'** (9:119). And the Prophet encouraged truthfulness and said, '*Adhere to truthfulness, because truthfulness leads to goodness, and goodness leads to Paradise. And a person will continue to be truthful, and strive to be truthful until he will be written down with God as a truthful person.*' And he warned against falsehood, and said, '*Beware of falsehood, because falsehood leads to wickedness, and wickedness leads to the Fire. And a person will continue lying, and striving to lie until he is written down with God as a great liar.*' O my brother Muslims, O youth, be true in your sayings with your brothers, and with those non-Muslims whom you live amongst."[47]

ᘓ

This is the reality of Islām which places tremendous emphasis and value on honouring one's contracts and agreements and having just, kind dealings with everybody irrespective of creed or race.

Likewise, Islām nurtures individuals to the peak of perfection in nobility of character.

---

[46] This is a reference to the extremists—who are discussed in a later chapter—and whose ideas are found today among groups such as Hizb ut-Taḥrīr, al-Muhājirūn, al-Qaeda, ISIS and others and individuals such as the likes of Abū Ḥamzah and Abū Qatādah.

[47] A recorded word of advice delivered on 28th July 2000. This advice has been repeatedly disseminated to Muslim audiences in the West for the past eighteen years to serve as a reminder of their obligations and duties and as a refutation of extremists and sympathesizers of terrorists such as the likes of Anjem Choudary and his small band of followers.

Perfection of Character

Perfection of character—through monotheism, righteous works and observance of law—was the purpose of the message of the Prophet (ﷺ). He stated in a famous authentic tradition: "*I have not been sent except for the completion and perfection of noble manners.*"[48] He also said: "*The most perfect of believers in faith are those with the best manners and the best of you are those who are best to their wives.*"[49] He also said: "*[The whole of] righteousness is [but] noble manners.*"[50] He also said: "*There is nothing placed on the scales [of righteous deeds] weightier than good manners.*"[51] Hence, the status of good manners is lofty in Islām and is one of its primary aims.

Just as Jesus (عَلَيۡهِ ٱلسَّلَامُ) called to the worship of only one Lord, to righteous works and to adherence to the law as the only means of salvation and reward after the grace and mercy of God, Prophet Muḥammad (ﷺ) called to the very same message. This is because what he conveyed came from **the same source** as the teachings of all the Prophets, having the same foundations and objective, which is the rectification of the servant and the land.

However, there is no moral and behavioural code which draws out perfection in human character in a more complete way than the code of Islām. If Muslims were to truly act upon this guidance, they would receive recognition and praise, as they often did in past centuries, when even warring enemies had to concede their moral and ethical superiority.

Perhaps the best way to illustrate this is through examples that can be drawn from the book, "*The Preaching of Islam*", by the British Orientalist scholar and historian, **Thomas Walker Arnold** (d. 1930).[52]

---

[48] Ṣaḥīḥ al-Jāmiʿ al-Ṣaghīr (no. 2349).
[49] Ṣaḥīḥ al-Jāmiʿ al-Ṣaghīr (no. 1232).
[50] Related by Muslim (no. 4633).
[51] Ṣaḥīḥ al-Targhīb wal-Tarhīb (no. 2641).
[52] Sir Thomas Walker Arnold (d. 1930) was a knighted British orientalist scholar and historian of Islamic Art who wrote this book which documents the spread of Islām across the East and West. Drawing upon hundreds of resources written in more than ten languages, including those from centres of Orientalism in Europe, Arnold provides a picture different from that of

First of all, let us start with Arnold writing about the effect of a 9th century Muslim scholar on non-Muslim citizens. He wrote: "On the other hand, the influence of the more orthodox doctors of Islam in the conversion of unbelievers is attested by the tradition that twenty thousand Christians, Jews and Magians became Muslims when the great Imām Ibn Ḥanbal died."[53]

Jews and Christians recognised the role of Muslim scholars in encouraging and admonishing their rulers to abide by justice and fairness with their subjects and as a result, non-Muslims received justice, moderation and tolerance. They would also witness the tremendous piety and nobility in character of Muslim scholars which deeply affected and moved them. **Imām Aḥmad bin Ḥanbal** (d. 855) was one such scholar and he was respected and revered greatly by non-Muslims and Muslims alike. He was treated by a Christian physician once. When the Christian entered upon him, he said: "I have desired to see you for many years. Your presence is not only rectification for the people of Islām, but for the whole of creation. There is to be found none amongst our Christian associates except that he is pleased with you."[54]

---

modern loons and rabid Islām haters, who, on ideological grounds and whims of the soul, spread lies about Islām and Muslims. As this book predates the modern era, it is free of inherent bias on grounds of geopolitics. It is free of agendas such as those of **neoconservative war-mongers**, **corporate terrorists** and **ideologues** such as Samuel Huntington and Bernard Lewis who provided academic and intellectual fuel for the false clash of civilisations narrative. This narrative was designed to provide justification for the planned invasions and wars in the Middle East by presenting Islām and Muslims as inherently backward and violent. This ideological and military assault has been to the serious detriment of the people of those lands such as Afghanistan, Irāq, Syria, Libya and others as well as the inhabitants of Western nations who have to bear the economic, political and security consequences of these invasions and wars. These geopolitical machinations are for the benefit of corporate terrorists and the owners of private international banks who hold sway over governments, and not for the benefit of the ordinary citizens.

[53] *The Preaching of Islam* (London Constable & Company, 1913), p.74-75. The tradition referred to is well established through noted and prominent trustworthy authorities and is documented in both works of history and biography. From such authorities is Abū Ḥātim al-Rāzī (d. 891). Refer to *al-Bidāyah wal-Nihāyah* of Ibn Kathīr (10/342).

[54] In the Musnad of Imām Aḥmad (p. 79) with checking of Aḥmad Shākir.

Numerous reports indicate that the funeral of Imām Aḥmad was attended by over one million people and this had a deep impact on the Jews, Christians and Magians who were also in attendance. Seeing the effect of the teachings of the Qurʾān upon the character of Muslims, especially their righteous scholars, these thousands accepted Islām, willingly, without compulsion. Regrettably, this is a side of Islām that many non-Muslims have never seen or experienced[55] but which throughout history, even the most hostile of enemies have been forced to acknowledge.

Next, we can provide numerous examples that Arnold gives of the recognition—even by warring enemies—of Muslim religious, moral and ethical superiority, even during times of conflict.

1. Arnold recounts a story from the second Crusade told by Odo of Deuil, a monk and chaplain of Louis VII of France, in which the pilgrim Crusaders suffered a disastrous defeat at the hands of Muslims in 1148 CE on their way to Jerusalem through Attalia, which is southwest Turkey today. Those pilgrims who could afford the exhorbitant demands of Greek merchants—who were their fellow Christians—were able to take ship to Antioch. However, the majority of them, including the sick and wounded were at the mercy of the Greeks who had been paid by Louis VII of France to provide escort for these pilgrims and look after their sick until they were strong enough to move on. When the bulk of the army had left, the Greek Christians acted treacherously towards their brethren in faith and directed the Muslims to those large numbers who still remained behind. In an ensuing battle, a party of three to four hundred thousand attempted to escape, but were surrounded, and were about to be annihilated completely. Arnold cites the story as told by Odo of Deuil: "The situation of the survivors would have been utterly hopeless, had not the sight of their misery melted the hearts of the Muhammadans [Muslims] to pity. They tended the sick and relieved the poor and starving with open-handed liberality. Some even bought up the French money which

---

[55] Partly because Muslims do not live up to and exemplify the lofty ideals of Islām as they ought to and have become more inclined to the world and its glitter, or are engrossed in deviations from Islām in belief and practice, or are disobedient to God and His Messenger through crime and vice.

the Greeks had got out of the pilgrims by force or cunning, and lavishly distributed it among the needy. **So great was the contrast between the kind treatment the pilgrims received from the unbelievers [Muslims] and the cruelty of their fellow-Christians, the Greeks, who imposed forced labour upon them, beat them and robbed them of what little they had left, that many of them voluntarily embraced the faith of their deliverers.**"[56]

2. Speaking of the Christians of the Byzantine empire, Arnold wrote: "They therefore readily—and even eagerly—received the new masters [Muslims] who promised them religious toleration, and were willing to compromise their religious position and their national independence if only they could free themselves from the immediately impending danger. **The people of Emessa closed the gates of their city against the army of Heraclius and told the Muslims that they preferred their government and justice to the injustice and oppression of the Greeks.**"[57]

3. Speaking of the Christians of Syria and Jordan, Arnold cites a letter written by Christians to the Arabs: "**O Muslims, we prefer you to the Byzantines, though they are of our own faith, because you keep better faith with us and are more merciful to us and refrain from doing us injustice and your rule over us is better than theirs, for they have robbed us of our goods and our homes.**" and then himself observes: "Emessa, Arethusa, Hieropolis and other towns entered into treaties whereby they became tributary to the Arabs... **Further, the self-restraint of the conquerers and the humanity which they displayed in their campaigns, must have excited profound respect and secured a welcome for an invading army that was guided by such principles of justice and moderation as were laid down by the Caliph Abu Bakr...**"[58]

4. Arnold also discusses the recognition by Christian writers of the more recent past of the superiority of Muslims in religious observance, devotion and ethical conduct. He recounts how they praised Muslims, "**... for the earnestness and intensity of their**

---

[56] *The Preaching of Islam* (1896), Westminster: Archibald Constable and Co. pp. 75-76.

[57] Ibid. p. 44

[58] Ibid. p. 49.

religious life; their zeal in the performance of the observances prescribed by their faith; the outward decency and modesty displayed in their apparel and mode of living; the absence of ostentatious display and the simplicity of life observable even in the great and powerful." He also cites from an Alexander Ross, who despite his dislike of Islām, was honest enough to admit: "... if Christians will but diligently read and observe the laws and histories of the Mahometans [Muslims], they may blush to see **how zealous they are in the works of devotion, piety, and charity, how devout, cleanly, and reverend in their mosques; how careful are they to observe their hours of prayer five times a day wherever they are, or however employed. How constantly do they observe their fasts from morning till night a whole month together; how loving and charitable the Muslemans [Muslims] are to each other, and how careful [i.e. caring] of strangers may be seen by their hospitals, both for the poor and for travellers; if we observe their justice, temperance, and other moral virtues, we may truly blush at our own coldness, both in devotion and charity, at our injustice, intemperance, and oppression; doubtless these men will rise up in judgment against us; and surely their devotion, piety and works of mercy are main causes of the growth of Mahometism [Islām].**"[59]

5. Speaking about why Islām spread so easily across Africa and Asia, Arnold explains the condition of African and Asian religion whose doctors had, "substituted abstruse metaphysical dogmas for the religion of Christ: they tried to combat the licentiousness of the age by setting forth the celestial merit of celibacy and the angelic excellence of virginity—seclusion from the world was the road of holiness, dirt was the characteristic of monkish sanctity—the people were practically polytheists, worshipping a crowd of martyrs, saints and angels; the upper classes were effeminate and corrupt, the middle classes oppressed by taxation, the slaves without hope for the present or the future..." Arnold then states: "**Islam swept away this mass of corruption and superstition.** It was a revolt against empty theological polemics; it was a masculine protest against the exaltation of celibacy as a crown of piety. It brought out the fundamental dogmas of religion—the unity and

---

[59] *The Preaching of Islam* (1913, 2nd edition), p.74-75.

greatness of God, that He is merciful and righteous, that He claims obedience to His will, resignation and faith. It proclaimed the responsibility of man, a future life, a day of judgment, and stern retribution to fall upon the wicked; and enforced the duties of prayer, almsgiving, fasting and benevolence. **It thrust aside the artificial virtues, the religious frauds and follies, the perverted moral sentiments, and the verbal subtleties of theological disputants. It replaced monkishness by manliness. It gave hope to the slave, brotherhood to mankind, and recognition to the fundamental facts of human nature.**"[60]

These are only some examples from Arnold's book alone and there are hundreds more that could be extracted from other non-Muslim sources. The intent behind them is to show that the pillars, commands and prohibitions of Islām and its morality and ethics have been shown to nurture human character to a level of perfection that is—even if unwillingly—recognised by enemies and foes, even in the midst of conflict and war, and whose factual realities, even the most bigoted and hateful cannot dismiss. It is from this angle that one can appreciate why Islām is winning large numbers and rapidly growing through conversions, despite all of the immense negativity. Those who interact with devout, upright Muslims who are upon an orthodox understanding of Islām find great disparity between how Muslims are presented in the media and what they have directly learned and personally experienced with Muslims.

It is important to note that not all Muslim individuals, societies or nations may exhibit the types of ethics and qualities which have been exemplified above. To take drug-dealers, pimps, groomers, murderers, oppressors, extremists, terrorists and the injustices of localised cultural traditions as examples of what Islām is and what it calls to is from profound ignorance or pure dishonesty.

After our discussion of ethics, just dealings and perfection of character, we move to the subject of **race** and **colour**.

---

[60] *The Preaching of Islam* (1913, 2nd edition), p.71-72.

Race and Colour

The children of Adam have been honoured and preferred over all of God's creatures due to what He bestowed upon them of the ability to know, think, reflect, reason, choose and act and due to the favours, facilities and enjoyments He has granted to them:

وَلَقَدْ كَرَّمْنَا بَنِي آدَمَ وَحَمَلْنَاهُمْ فِي الْبَرِّ وَالْبَحْرِ وَرَزَقْنَاهُم مِّنَ الطَّيِّبَاتِ وَفَضَّلْنَاهُمْ عَلَىٰ كَثِيرٍ مِّمَّنْ خَلَقْنَا تَفْضِيلًا

"And We have certainly honored the children of Adam and carried them on the land and sea and provided for them of the good things and preferred them over much of what We have created, with [definite] preference." (17:70).

God also made them into tribes and nations for wisdoms:

يَا أَيُّهَا النَّاسُ إِنَّا خَلَقْنَاكُم مِّن ذَكَرٍ وَأُنثَىٰ وَجَعَلْنَاكُمْ شُعُوبًا وَقَبَائِلَ لِتَعَارَفُوا إِنَّ أَكْرَمَكُمْ عِندَ اللَّهِ أَتْقَاكُمْ إِنَّ اللَّهَ عَلِيمٌ خَبِيرٌ

"O mankind! We have created you from a male and a female, and made you into nations and tribes, that you may know one another. Indeed, the most noble of you in the sight of God (Allāh) is the most righteous of you." (49:13).

The Muslim Scholar, **'Abd al-Raḥmān al-Sa'dī** (d. 1956) said: "They all return to Adam and Eve... and He made them into nations and tribes so that they may know each other. If each soul had been made independent [from others] then the mutual aid, cooperation, inheritance and fulfilment of the rights of relatives would not have been possible, so He made them into nations and tribes so that they can attain these affairs..."[61]

The renowned Muslim scholar **Muḥammad al-Amīn al-Shanqīṭī** (d. 1973) said: "The statement of the Exalted: '**We have created you from a male and a female**' indicated the equality of all people in their origin— because their father is one and their mother is one— this being the greatest reprimand of boasting about lineage and the insolence of some over others. After it, the Exalted made clear

---

[61] *Taysīr al-Karīm al-Raḥmān* (Cairo:Dār al-Ḥadīth) p. 893.

that He made them into nations and tribes so that they may become mutually acquainted with each other and that they can be distinguished from each other. Not that they may boast and become insolent towards each other. And this indicates that some of them being more noble than others must be on account of some other cause besides lineage."[62] That cause is following the guidance of the Messengers of God which is founded upon pure monotheism coupled with adherence to law and righteous works.

Diversity in colour and language is merely **a sign** amongst the signs of God:

وَمِنْ آيَاتِهِ خَلْقُ السَّمَاوَاتِ وَالْأَرْضِ وَاخْتِلَافُ أَلْسِنَتِكُمْ وَأَلْوَانِكُمْ إِنَّ فِي ذَٰلِكَ لَآيَاتٍ لِّلْعَالِمِينَ

"**And of His signs is the creation of the heavens and the earth and the diversity of your languages and your colours. Indeed in that are signs for those of knowledge**." (30:22).

Therefore, race and colour do not signify inherent superiority or inferiority of any race. As such, there is no tribalism or racism in Islam and superiority is not by complexion, tribe or nationality, but by individual piety and character:

إِنَّ أَكْرَمَكُمْ عِندَ ٱللَّهِ أَتْقَىٰكُمْ

Indeed, the most noble of you in the sight of God (Allāh) is the most righteous of you." (49:13).

The Prophet (ﷺ) said: "*An Arab has no superiority over a non-Arab nor a non-Arab has any superiority over an Arab. Also a white has no superiority over a black. Nor does a black have any superiority over a white except by piety.*"[63] And in another report: "*O people! Verily your Lord is One and your father [Adam] is one. An Arab has no superiority over a non-Arab, and a non-Arab has no superiority over an Arab. A red man has no superiority over a black man and a black man has no superiority over a red man except by piety.*"[64] He (ﷺ) also said: "*Verily, God does not look at your appearances and belongings but He*

---

[62] *Aḍwā' al-Bayān* (5/170).
[63] Al-Albānī in *Sharḥ al-Taḥāwiyyah*, p. 361.
[64] Ahmad in *al-Musnad* (no. 22978) and *al-Silsilah al-Ṣāhīḥah* (6/449).

looks at your hearts and your deeds."[65] The Prophet overturned and rooted out the deeply-embedded spirit of tribalism, ancestral pride and racism from Pre-Islāmic Arabia through God's guidance in just two decades and made it a lasting legacy till this day.[66]

The effects of these teachings and their influence on racist ideas and beliefs can be observed through the experience of Malcolm X whose bitter racial animosities against whites due to four hundred years of racism against blacks **was dissolved in an instant** during his pilgrimage to Mecca in 1964.

He wrote of his experience: "Never have I witnessed such sincere hospitality and overwhelming spirit of true brotherhood as is practiced by people of all colors and races here in this Ancient Holy Land, the home of Abraham, Muhammad and all the other Prophets of the Holy Scriptures. For the past week, I have been utterly speechless and spellbound by the graciousness I see displayed all around me by people of all colors... There were tens of thousands of pilgrims, from all over the world. They were of all colors, from blue-eyed blondes to black-skinned Africans. But we were all participating in the same ritual, displaying a spirit of unity and brotherhood that my experiences in America had led me to believe never could exist between the white and non-white. America needs to understand Islam, because this is the one religion that erases from its society the race problem... You may be shocked by these words coming from me. But on this pilgrimage, what I have seen, and experienced, has forced me to re-arrange much of my thought-patterns previously held, and to toss aside some of my previous conclusions. This was not too difficult for me. Despite my firm convictions, I have always been a man who tries to face facts, and to accept the reality of life as new experience and new knowledge unfolds it. I have always kept an open mind, which is

---

[65] Related by Muslim (no. 2564).

[66] Any overt or hidden racism on behalf of individual Muslims, rulers or ruled, in the past or the present has no connection to Islām and is completely antithetical to it. In a similar manner, the blatant racism and disdain of other races that were behind the entire European colonialist enterprise for hundreds of years in which hundreds of millions were killed has no connection with Jesus (عَلَيْهِ السَّلَام) and his teachings.

necessary to the flexibility that must go hand in hand with every form of intelligent search for truth. During the past eleven days here in the Muslim world, I have eaten from the same plate, drunk from the same glass, and slept in the same bed (or on the same rug)—while praying to the same God—with fellow Muslims, whose eyes were the bluest of blue, whose hair was the blondest of blond, and whose skin was the whitest of white... Never have I been so highly honored. Never have I been made to feel more humble and unworthy."[67]

☙

So far, we have discussed the fiṭrah which places all humans on an equal footing from birth, and this is the foundation for Islām. It is natural for a person to perceive that there is a greater power and authority behind what is observed of the natural phenomena and what is experienced of innumerable benefits through the systems of cause and effect in creation. This leads to the issue of singling out this Creator for gratitude and worship being the greatest form of justice from which all other manifestations of justice arise. From here the pillars of Islām such as prayer, fasting and charity, the emphasised obligations, the prohibitions, the inculcation of moral excellence, ethical behaviour and perfection in character lead to rectification of both the servant and the land. Islām maximises goodness and rectification and minimises evil and corruption in society—in all realms—whether personal, societal or economic.

However, there are dangers that can harm society if they are left to take root. From them is unchecked **religious fervour** that leads to extremism and exaggeration in religion. God revealed knowledge of this affair and its grave danger upon the Muslim nation to His Prophet (صَلَّى ٱللَّٰهُ عَلَيْهِ وَسَلَّمَ) and we shall discuss this matter in what follows.

---

[67] *Letter From Mecca*, April 1964. From *Autobiography of Malcolm X* by Alex Haley (1992).

Religious Fervour and Exaggeration

Unchecked religious fervour that leads to exaggeration in religion is prohibited and comprises misguidance. The Prophet (ﷺ) said: "*The extremists have perished, the extremists have perished, the extremists have perished.*"[68] And he also said: "*Beware of exaggeration in religion. That which destroyed those who came before you was their exaggeration in religion.*"[69] As such, going to extremes, exaggerating in worship, abstinence and delving deeply into religion through speculation, conjecture and the likes are all prohibited and from the ways of corruption and misguidance.

Previous nations are criticised in the Qur'ān for falling into exaggeration on account of religious fervour:

يَا أَهْلَ الْكِتَابِ لَا تَغْلُوا فِي دِينِكُمْ وَلَا تَقُولُوا عَلَى اللَّهِ إِلَّا الْحَقَّ

"O People of the Book do not go to excesses in your religion and say not of God (Allāh) but the truth." (4:171).

The Prophet (ﷺ) once reprimanded three men. One had vowed to pray the whole night every night. Another vowed to fast continuously each day and a third vowed to remain celibate for the rest of his days. He censured them and informed them that he only prays some of the night, fasts voluntarily some days and not others and also marries. He then told them: "*Whoever leaves my way [of moderation] is not of me.*"[70]

Thus, exaggerating, creating burdens and imposing shackles upon oneself and others through these means is forbidden and is from the ways that led previous nations to ruin. An illustration of this is the **monasticism and celibacy** that some Christians imposed upon themselves. However, many of them were unable abide by it for long because it opposes the fundamental facts and realities of human nature. The Qur'ān speaks of the monasticism and celibacy they invented:

---

[68] Reported by Muslim (no. 2670).
[69] Ṣaḥīḥ Sunan al-Nasā'ī (2/640) of al-Albānī.
[70] In a tradition related by al-Bukhārī (no. 5063) and Muslim (no. 1401).

وَرَهْبَانِيَّةً ابْتَدَعُوهَا مَا كَتَبْنَاهَا عَلَيْهِمْ إِلَّا ابْتِغَاءَ رِضْوَانِ اللَّهِ فَمَا رَعَوْهَا حَقَّ رِعَايَتِهَا فَآتَيْنَا الَّذِينَ آمَنُوا مِنْهُمْ أَجْرَهُمْ وَكَثِيرٌ مِّنْهُمْ فَاسِقُونَ

"**And the monasticism, they devised it [and imposed it upon themselves] whilst we did not prescribe upon them but to seek the pleasure of God (Allāh). However, they did not observe [their self-imposed monasticism] with true observance. We gave those who believed among them [and observed it dutifully] their due reward. But most of them are disobedient sinners.**" (57:27).

Similarly, among the Jews were those who went to extremes in their religion by imposing the shackles of invented observances, statutes and laws upon those beneath them. This led to a form of despotic micro-management by religious leaders of the lives of ordinary Jews. Those who came after began to distort and alter the law in order to lighten burdens and find loopholes.

God does not impose hardships that lead to corruption in morals and character. Thus, Islāmic law is in moderation between the neglect of Christians who made the law of non-effect in salvation and the extremism of Jews who exaggerated in it. Islām removed the various shackles that had been imposed in matters of law and brought ease. God (Allāh) said in the Qurʾān:

وَمَا جَعَلَ عَلَيْكُمْ فِي الدِّينِ مِنْ حَرَجٍ

"**He has not placed upon you in the religion any difficulty.**" (22:78).

Muslims who faithfully follow the companions of the Prophet (ﷺ) in their understanding and application of the texts strongly oppose this type of exaggeration in belief, worship, observance of law and conduct. Hence, in early Islāmic history, Muslim scholars opposed rebellious sects like the **Khārijites**—precursors to al-Qaeda and ISIS—and the **Rāfiḍite Shīʿites.** Both of these sects were **a political revolution** against Islām and its leadership, driven by ignorance, misguided zeal, extremism and exaggeration **mixed with worldly grievances**. This leads us to a very necessary discussion of **extremism**, its origins and causes.

Extremism: Origins and Causes

Ignorance and **exaggeration** lead to extremism. These two traits are a dangerous combination and are censured in Islām. The first extremists to appear among Muslims possessing these two traits were known as the **Khārijites** or *renegade extremists* who unleashed terrorism against the Muslim nation. They are the ideological ancestors of al-Qaeda, ISIS and similar groups today. They combined worldly grievances with ignorance of Islām, the Qurʾān and its injunctions. There is a well-known model for their appearance and deviation. Muslim scholars have spoken, written and warned against it **for over 1400 years** from the time of Ibn ʿAbbās (رَضِيَ ٱللَّهُ عَنْهُ)—the most learned of the Qurʾānic scholars from the Prophet's disciples who refuted the extremists' misinterpretation of the Qurʾān—to the present day.

Their nucleus consisted of a group of hypocrites in the time of the Prophet (صَلَّى ٱللَّهُ عَلَيْهِ وَسَلَّمَ) who were unhappy about not receiving a share in the distribution of charities. They were mentioned in the Qurʾān:

وَمِنْهُم مَّن يَلْمِزُكَ فِي الصَّدَقَاتِ فَإِنْ أُعْطُوا مِنْهَا رَضُوا وَإِن لَّمْ يُعْطَوْا مِنْهَا إِذَا هُمْ يَسْخَطُونَ

"And among them [the Hypocrites] are some who criticize you concerning the [distribution of] charities. If they are given from them, they approve; but if they are not given from them, at once they become angry." (9:68).

They accused the Prophet and later his companions of not judging by justice and of engaging in monopoly and class distinction.[71] They later assassinated two of his close friends—ʿUthman and ʿAlī (رَضِيَ ٱللَّهُ عَنْهُمَا). They were his two sons-in-law and the third and fourth leaders of the Muslim nation respectively. Their appearance as **an insurgency** was prophesied by the Prophet (صَلَّى ٱللَّهُ عَلَيْهِ وَسَلَّمَ) after they revealed their discontent and exposed their ill intentions during

[71] They can be likened to Marxist, Communist revolutionaries claiming to fight the tyranny of capital and class distinction, but in reality seeking power. They clothed their worldly motivations with religious rhetoric.

his time. He specifically mentioned the location of their appearance (Iraq) as an insurgency, the time and circumstances of their emergence as a separate body (during a civil war), and who would eventually fight and kill them (ʿAlī, the fourth caliph).

He also mentioned that they would continue to plague the Muslim nation till the end of time and commanded Muslim authorities to fight and kill them.

The traditions regarding the Khārijites are well known in the books dealing with Qurʾānic interpretation (*tafsīr*), Islāmic theology (*ʿaqīdah*), heretical sects (*firaq*) and history (*tārīkh*).

When they appeared as an insurgent group twenty-five years after the Prophet (صَلَّى ٱللَّٰهُ عَلَيْهِ وَسَلَّمَ), they claimed that the rulers of the time, ʿUthmān and ʿAlī (رَضِيَ ٱللَّٰهُ عَنْهُمَا), had judged with injustice, had abandoned God's law, left Islām and had to be removed. They held that so long as such leaders were in power, **Islām was non-existent** and that redemption lay in forcefully removing them and re-establishing Islām once again as they claimed. They alleged that anyone who did not expel these rulers from Islām had shown loyalty to them and was thereby also a non-Muslim, an apostate. They then **reframed jihād as the struggle against leaders** and also developed a new, innovated jurisprudence for interacting with the rest of the Muslims whom they considered unbelievers.

After assassinating ʿUthmān (رَضِيَ ٱللَّٰهُ عَنْهُ) in 656 CE and engineering a civil war, they abandoned the main body of Muslims ruled by ʿAlī (رَضِيَ ٱللَّٰهُ عَنْهُ) and took up arms against them. Over a period of two years, they mobilised the ignorant rabble to their cause through slogans and tactics of propaganda. They used these means to recruit them into **their breakaway Islāmic state** at Nahrawān, a place that was just south of Baghdād in Iraq. During this time period they started slaughtering Muslims on the basis of this extremist ideology.

Their first victims were the Prophet's companion ʿAbd Allāh bin Khabbāb (رَضِيَ ٱللَّٰهُ عَنْهُ) and the women of his household, one of whom was heavily pregnant. They slaughtered him on the banks of the Euphrates and then went on to slaughter his whole household, including the pregnant woman and her unborn. Their justification being that ʿAbd Allāh did not agree with their excommunication and disavowal of ʿAlī, and hence was no longer a Muslim.

They justified their sedition and terrorism through the slogans of *Social Justice*, *Jihād*, *God's Law*, *Enjoining Good and Prohibiting Evil* and *Redemption*. The specific set of ideas, events and circumstances and the motives leading to their separation and congregation as a military force represent a clear model to which the appearance of ISIS (Daesh) in the 21st century and all Khārijite movements in history can be compared. **A clear resemblance will be found each time**. The closest example outside of Islām for these extremists are the Marxist, Communist revolutionaries who—using the slogans of *social justice* and the *tyranny of capital*—instigate and mobilise the masses to revolution and topple the authorities. After wrestling power, they mercilessly slaughter anyone who is even the slightest threat to them and their grip of power. The Khārijite extremists clothe these same ideas and activities with religious rhetoric and misapplication of texts. They are but ignorant worshippers with insincere intentions. They feign piety whilst being motivated by the world, and they speak with alluring speech that amazes and deceives the young, naive and ignorant.

From the authentically related statements of the Prophet (صَلَّى ٱللَّهُ عَلَيْهِ وَسَلَّمَ) about this group include the following: "*They will depart from the religion (Islām) like an arrow passes through its game and they do not return back to it until the arrow returns back to its bow-string*" and "*Their faith will not pass beyond their throats*" and "*They will recite the Qur'ān but it will not go beyond their collar-bones*," indicating ignorance and false scholarship.

The Prophet also said, "*They will speak with the best speech of the creation*," meaning, beautified, alluring speech, and "*(They are) young of age, foolish of mind*" and "*Their speech is beautiful, alluring yet their actions are evil*" and "*They are the most evil of the creation*" and "*They call to the Book of God, yet they have nothing to do with it*."

The Prophet (صَلَّى ٱللَّهُ عَلَيْهِ وَسَلَّمَ) went further and also said "*They are the most evil of those killed beneath the canopy of the sky*" and "*They are the Dogs of Hellfire*."[72] The Prophet also signalled his intent to kill them

[72] These reports can be found in the ḥadīth collections of al-Bukhārī, Muslim, Abū Dāwūd, Ibn Mājah and others and are well known and famous to the Scholars of the Muslims and the students of knowledge.

should he have reached them.[73] He said "*If I was to reach them, I would slaughter them, like the slaughtering of ʿĀd (a destroyed nation of the past),*" meaning, every last one of them until not one of them remains as explained by the renowned scholar, Ibn Ḥajar al-ʿAsqalānī (d. 1449) in his commentary on this tradition.[74]

He also mentioned their appearance in later times: "*There will appear at the end of time a people who are young of age, foolish-minded. They will speak with the best (and most-alluring) of speech (that is spoken) by people and will recite the Qurʾān but it will not go beyond their throats. They will pass out of Islām as the arrow passes through its game. Whoever meets them, let him kill them, for there is a reward for whoever kills them.*"[75] In these texts, the Prophet actually incited his nation—under the command of the authorities—to kill them.

Recognising them as the very ones alluded to in these Prophetic traditions, ʿAlī (رَضِيَ اللَّهُ عَنْهُ), the Prophet's cousin and son-in-law, fought and defeated their army of thousands in 659 CE, anticipating the great reward mentioned by the Prophet for killing these terrorists. Their breakaway alleged "Islāmic State" was disbanded but ten of the terrorists escaped and fled to various lands and preserved this ideology which is why it remains till the present day. Out of bloodthirsty revenge, a terrorist known as **Bin Muljam** assassinated ʿAlī (رَضِيَ اللَّهُ عَنْهُ) in 661 CE. Two of his associates tried to simultaneously assassinate the Muslim rulers in Syria and Egypt—Muʿāwiyah and ʿAmr bin al-ʿĀṣ, both companions of the Prophet —but they failed.

It is interesting to note that the terrorists appeared **during a time of civil and political strife** after they had assassinated ʿUthmān (رَضِيَ اللَّهُ عَنْهُ), the third caliph and the Prophet's son-in-law. They took advantage of this situation to gather, organise and recruit followers. Revolutions, civil war and the likes are their breeding grounds. This is exactly how ISIS appeared in Iraq and Syria after invasions of these countries—orchestrated by neoconservative warmongers and corporate vultures—left vacuums of power to

---

[73] For documentation of these traditions refer *to Jāmiʾ al-Uṣūl Fī Aḥādīth al-Rasūl* of Ibn al-Athīr (10/76-92) under the heading of "*The Khārijites.*"

[74] Refer to *Fatḥ al-Bārī* (6/435).

[75] Reported by Ibn Mājah (no. 167).

which the extremists flocked after the so-called "Arab Spring" revolutions. They took advantage of this political turmoil to gather and mobilise in a manner that was not possible for them prior to that. Just like their ideological forefathers—the very first Khārijite extremists—they use slick emotional propaganda to recruit the ignorant and foolish from every nation.

When they gain power, they kill Muslims who do not agree with their ideology. Describing them, the late Salafi scholar **Muḥammad bin Ṣāliḥ al-ʿUthaymīn** (d. 2001) said: "If you were to look into the hearts [of the Khārijite extremists], you would find them black and hard. They accuse sinful Muslims of disbelief, but they are greater in disbelief."[76]

From the above, it is clear that the first Khārijite extremists were a revolution against Islam, its rulers and subjects and they are the foundation of all insurgent movements thereafter. They believe in the obligation of overthrowing Muslim authorities whom they accuse of injustice and tyranny and they encapsulate Islām around this one issue. In other words, Islām is about nothing but political authority (sulṭah). Toppling rulers to snatch power is the core activity by which redemption is sought. This is a gross distortion of Islām not known to any Prophet or Messenger of God. It was fabricated by the Khārijites of old and revived in the 20th century by thinkers—such as **Abū Aʿlā Mawdūdī** (d. 1979) and **Sayyid Quṭb** (d. 1966)—both of whom were influenced by European revolutionary ideologies which had uprooted the old monarchies.

It is a religious obligation upon the rulers of the Muslims to combat them, Muslim scholars to refute their ideology and for Muslims to expose them and warn against them. Their actions are pure terrorism and not jihād. Those who sympathise with them or defend them are ignorant, severely lacking in intellect and have a deficient understanding of Islām.

Consider what the Muslim scholar and jurist **Abu Bakr al-Ājurrī** (d. 970) said of these extremists in his book pertaining to Islāmic theology: "The scholars have not differed that the Khārijite

---

[76] *Liqāʾal-Bāb al-Maftūḥ* (no. 11).

(extremists) are an evil people, disobedient to God and His Messenger, even if they pray, fast and strive hard in worship. None of that will be beneficial to them. They proclaim the commanding of good and prohibiting of evil but that will not benefit them because they distort the Qurʾān upon their desires and deceive the Muslims. God, the Most High, warned us against them. The Prophet warned us against them. The Rightly-Guided Caliphs warned us against them. The Prophet's companions warned us against them. They are an evil, filthy despicable people."[77]

The famous Qurʾān commentator **Ibn Kathīr** (d. 1373) said, close to seven centuries ago: "If these [Khārijites] were to acquire strength, they would corrupt the entire earth in Irāq and Shām (Syria) and they would not leave a male or female child nor a man or woman (alive). This is because in their view the people (Muslims) have become corrupt in a way that nothing will rectify their (situation) except mass murder."[78] This is precisely what has happened with al-Qaeda and ISIS during the past decade.

Many scholars, past and present, consider these extremists to be apostates from Islām because they make lawful what God made unlawful—which is the killing of innocent people.

For example, the late Salafi scholar **ʿAbd al-ʿAzīz bin Bāz** (d. 1999) said of them: "That which is apparent from the Prophetic traditions is that they are disbelievers." He also said, after mentioning the view of the scholars who consider them only as sinful Muslims, "That which is correct is that they are disbelievers," citing as evidence the statement of the Prophet (صَلَّىٱللَّهُعَلَيْهِوَسَلَّمَ), "*If I was to reach them, I would slaughter them like the slaughtering of ʿĀd.*"[79] The people of ʿĀd were a nation of the past who belied their Prophet and were destroyed by a screaming, violent wind without a single survivor. The meaning of this well-known tradition is that had the Prophet reached these extremists and terrorists when they appeared he would have killed every single last one of them.

[77] In his book, *Al-Sharīʿah* (1/136).
[78] *Al-Bidāyah wal-Nihāyah* (10/585).
[79] A Prophetic tradition related by al-Bukhārī.

Shaykh Ibn Bāz then said, “The correct and apparent view from the textual evidences is that on account of their extremism, their expulsion of Muslims (from the fold of Islām) and declaring them to be eternal inhabitants of Hellfire, they are disbelievers.”[80]

Extremist elements like the Khārijites in Islām have parallels in **Judaism**, **Christianity**, **Hinduism** and **Buddhism**.

One can read the essay *18 Principles of Rebirth* as outlined by Avraham Stern—founder of the Jewish terrorist group Lehi, also known as the Stern Gang[81]—to identify this way of thinking which forms the basis of the activities of extremist Jews such as the **Haredis** , **Gush Emunim** and those within the **settler community**. Their ideology is parallel to the caliphate-centric ideology of ISIS, though it is based on the notion of **redemption on the basis of land**. Upon this doctrine, the extremists among them believe in the killing of non-combatant men, women and children and the confiscation of land and property without mercy as a means of redeeming land they believe is theirs by divine promise.[82]

Likewise, the Christian **Lord’s Resistance Army** which aims to rule Uganda upon Biblical law and has to date massacred 100,000 people, displaced millions and taken an estimated 60,000 child captives whom they use as soldiers. A toll much greater than that of al-Qaeda and ISIS combined but of which we have not heard much in the mainstream media.

In accordance with justice, Muslims do not paint all Jews and Christians with the same brush as extremists and terrorists such as **Baruch Goldstein**[83] and **Anders Breivik**[84] and their likes. Most Jews

---

[80] http://www.binbaz.org.sa/mat/20688.

[81] An extremist Zionist organisation that waged a campaign of terror against the British in Palestine during the mid to late 1940s. They assassinated Lord Moyne, Count Folke Bernadette and also plotted to assassinate Ernest Bevin (British Foreign Secretary) and Winston Churchill (Prime Minister).

[82] Professor Israel Shahak’s *Jewish Fundamentalism in Israel* (Pluto Press, 2004) is an eye-opening read on the role and influence of Jewish religious extremists and racial supremacists such as Gush Emunim and the Haredis in the politics of the region.

[83] A Jewish settler who in February 1994 walked into a mosque in Hebron and killed 29 people whilst they were praying the dawn prayer.

and Christians reject the actions of these extremists and also provide explanations as to why their religious texts do not sanction their actions.

It is the goal of ⇨

- hardline political and religious ultra-Zionists[85]
- evangelical Christian fundamentalists,
- far-right nationalist movements which often have tinges of white supremacist or racist ideology,
- unscrupulous academics,
- and money-hungry self-styled "terrorism experts"[86]

⇨ to present the ideology of these Khārijite extremists as the embodiment of Islām itself. This is patently false.

It is like saying that the message of Jesus is embodied in the actions of Anders Breivik, Timothy McVeigh and the Klu Klux Klan, and that the message of Moses is embodied in the actions of Baruch Goldstein, the Irgun and the Stern Gang and those Jewish "price tag" settler terrorists who firebomb houses during the night whilst women and children are sleeping in them.

There is much more to the teachings of those Prophets than the political ideologies of these extremists and terrorists and the grievances upon which they are founded.

---

[84] A Christian Islām hater and far-right Zionist who in July 2011 slaughtered over 70 people attending a youth camp on an Island in Norway. Almost all of them were teenagers and future members of a political party that is very sympathetic to the cause of the Palestinians.

[85] Not all Jews are Zionists and not all Zionists are Jews. A large number of Christians, particularly in America, are Zionists. Further, many religious Jews **vehemently reject** the claim of the Zionists that they speak for all Jews.

[86] There are many unscrupulous academics, journalists and personalities who have jumped on the financially lucrative bandwagon of peddling lies, distortions and hatred against Islām and indirectly, against Muslims. Many have found publishing online—whether in the form of videos for advertising revenue, or print and ebook format—as a lucrative source of income. The vast majority of non-Muslims are not informed enough to see through the lies and deceptions used in their rhetoric. And often, the motives of such people will be hidden and unclear because they may bring genuine issues of concern as the bait and hook—such as terrorism, crimes of a sexual nature committed by Muslims and the negative impact of immigration.

Jihād and Terrorism

The meaning of jihād in its broadest sense refers to personal effort and struggle by which a person strives to:

- remain devout and obedient to God,
- refrain from sins and transgressions and
- remain patient upon life's trials and difficulties.

The Prophet (ﷺ) said: "*The mujāhid (one engaged in jihād) is the one who struggles against his own soul in obedience to God.*"[87] It has many manifestations, both inward and outward. Benevolence to parents, raising children and speaking the truth, even if it is against oneself, are all manifestations of jihād.

From its manifestations is fighting (qitāl) behind the authority of the ruler within a regular army following the rule of law. This—as in all nations—is from the instruments of preserving national security. It refers to a conventional war between two parties that is fought justly, without treachery, and is always openly announced. Muslim jurists are agreed that it is performed under the ruler's authority and that all the affairs of war, peace, alliances, truces, covenants and diplomatic relations are strictly in the hands of the ruler. It is not permissible for any person to engage in fighting without the permission and authority of the ruler except in one case mentioned by the jurists: sudden attack by an enemy. This obviously requires immediate action from those in the vicinity before logistical command is taken by the military command and leadership of the state.

The famous Muslim jurist **Ibn Qudāmah** (d. 1223) said: "The affair of jihād is entrusted to the ruler and is under his consideration. It is binding upon the subjects to obey him in whatever he sees regarding it."[88] And the late Salafi scholar and jurist, **Muḥammad bin Ṣāliḥ al-'Uthaymīn** (d. 2001) said: "It is not permissible to engage in a military expedition with an army except with the permission of the ruler no matter what the situation. This is because it is the rulers who are addressed [in the texts] with the

---

[87] Related by Aḥmad, Ibn Ḥibbān and al-Ṭabarānī.

[88] *Al-Mughnī* (10/368).

affair of military expeditions and jihād and not individual citizens among the people. Individuals must follow the authorities."[89]

Further, war is not something primarily sought by Islām as it only takes the place of necessity. If a Muslim land is not attacked and no hostilities, barriers and hindrances are placed in front of the peaceful practice, proclamation and conveyance of Islām, then there is no legislation of jihad. In fact, the jihād of fighting is legislated as a necessity (ḍurūrah), as an emergency measure for the protection of the instrument of peaceful preaching as textually stated by the Muslim scholar, Ibn Taymiyyah (d. 1328).[90]

The contemporary Muslim scholar, **Shaykh Ṣāliḥ Āl al-Shaykh**, said: "The legislation [of Islām] is not desirous for war. Rather, war only takes the place of necessity. When the arena is open for invitation to God and conveying the message of God the Mighty and Majestic, then the foundation of jihād in the path of God is not legislated as has been said by Shaykh al-Islām Ibn Taymiyyah... He said that jihād has not been legislated except as [a means] to protect [the instrument of] peaceful invitation. When it is possible to convey the invitation [when hostility and hindrance are absent] then there is no angle for jihād. He gave evidences and known observations for that."[91]

The foundation lies in the following texts of the Qurʾān:

ادْعُ إِلَىٰ سَبِيلِ رَبِّكَ بِالْحِكْمَةِ وَالْمَوْعِظَةِ الْحَسَنَةِ وَجَادِلْهُم بِالَّتِي هِيَ أَحْسَنُ ۚ إِنَّ رَبَّكَ
هُوَ أَعْلَمُ بِمَن ضَلَّ عَن سَبِيلِهِ وَهُوَ أَعْلَمُ بِالْمُهْتَدِينَ

---

[89] *Sharḥ al-Mumtiʿ* (8/22). Muslim scholars are astute enough to note that the issue of jihād and the texts pertaining to it can be used by those motivated by political interests to work sedition. Shaykh al-ʿUthaymīn alludes to this on the same page: "A faction of people may make preparations [for battle] giving the impression that they desire the enemy whereas in reality, they desire to revolt against the ruler, or they may desire to transgress against another faction of people."

[90] Refer to the discussion by Ibn Taymiyyah (d. 1328) in his work *al-Jawāb al-Ṣaḥīḥ* (1/238, 240) in which he convincingly refutes the claim that the verses of fighting have abrogated the verses of peaceful preaching and argumentation. A discussion can be found in the article "*Terrorism is not Jihād*" which is available at www.islamagainstextremism.com.

[91] Refer to *Hādhā Huwa al-Islām* (p. 25).

"Invite to the way of your Lord with wisdom and good instruction, and argue with them in a way that is best. Indeed, your Lord is most knowing of who has strayed from His way, and He is most knowing of who is [rightly] guided." (16:125).

And also:

وَلَا تُجَادِلُوا أَهْلَ الْكِتَابِ إِلَّا بِالَّتِي هِيَ أَحْسَنُ إِلَّا الَّذِينَ ظَلَمُوا مِنْهُمْ

"And do not argue with the People of the Book except in a way that is best, save those who commit injustice among them..." (29:46).

The Qur'ānic exegete, **Imām al-Sa'dī** (d. 1956) stated: "The Exalted has prohibited disputing the People of the Scripture when it is done without insight and without any pleasingly acceptable principle. [It orders] that they should only argue in a way that is best: with good manners, gentleness and softness in speech; inviting to the truth; beautifying it; refuting the falsehood and censuring it and using the nearest of ways leading to it. [It explains] that the intent should not be mere argumentation in and of itself, desiring to dominate [others] and for love of exaltation. Rather, the intent should be to clarify the truth and guide the creation."[92]

These are decisive commands which will always remain in effect and they have not been abrogated at all.

The renowned scholar **Ibn Taymiyyah** (d. 1328) said: "What God the Exalted mentioned about argumentation with the People of the Book with that which is best—save those who commit injustice among them—is a decisive command which has not been abrogated by anything."[93]

He also said: "That it is known that fighting was only prescribed for a necessity (ḍurūrah) and had the people believed through evidences and signs [alone], fighting would not have been required."[94] He goes on to explain that in law, that which is legislated *as a necessity* cannot prevent that which is legislated *as an obligation*, namely, preaching and good argumentation.

---

[92] *Taysīr al-Karīm al-Raḥmān* (Beirut: Mu'assasah al-Risālah, 2002) p. 632.
[93] *Al-Jawāb al-Ṣaḥīḥ* (1/217).
[94] *Al-Jawāb al-Ṣaḥīḥ* (1/238).

He also said: "Fighting is only against the oppressor. For whoever fought the Muslims [on account of religion] can only be a transgressing oppressor."[95]

He also said: "Fighting is for the one who fights against us when we desire to proclaim the religion of God... so whoever did not prevent the Muslims from establishing the religion of God, then the harm of his unbelief is only upon himself."[96]

From the above, we learn that there is the ***jihād of defence*** which is legislated for the protection of borders and citizens. This is easy to grasp as every nation has the right to engage in defensive war for purposes of national security.

Examples of Islāmically legitimate jihāds supported by Western nations include the jihād against the Russian invasion of Afghanistan in the 1980s. Likewise, during the 1990s Western governments were rather indifferent to British citizens travelling to Bosnia to fight against the Serbians who committed atrocities against Muslims. They were not treated as terrorists, arrested, interrogated, charged and imprisoned. Likewise the war of Saudi Arabia and the Emirates against the Houthīs and Hizbollah proxies in Yemen who are trying to destabilise the region. Some Western powers support this war knowing full well that it has the legal ruling of a legitimate jihād in Islāmic law according to Muslim scholars both within and outside of Saudi Arabia.

Then there is the ***jihād of removing obstacles*** which is legislated due to necessity when hostilities and hindrances come in the way of peaceful practice, preaching, discussion and argumentation. When these circumstances exist, this jihād is legislated and this is the jihād alluded to in the statement of the Prophet (صَلَّى ٱللَّٰهُ عَلَيْهِ وَسَلَّمَ): "*I have been ordered to fight back against the people until they testify that none deserves to be worshipped but God...*"[97] Commenting on this tradition, the Muslim scholar Ibn Taymiyyah said: "His intent [in

---

[95] *Al-Jawāb al-Ṣaḥīḥ* (1/240).

[96] *Majmūʿ al-Fatāwā* (8/354).

[97] Reported by al-Bukhārī and Muslim. The verb qātala is used in this ḥadīth and is of the form fāʿala which carries the meaning of reciprocation. Thus, the fighting here is a response to fighting that has already been initiated.

this tradition] is fighting the wagers of war for whom God had granted permission [that they be fought back]. He did not intend [in this tradition] fighting those with a covenant and with respect to whom God had commanded the honouring of their covenant."[98]

This is precisely what the Prophet did. He fought back to remove obstacles of hindrance, aggression, violence and hostility so that people could freely and peacefully hear the message without distortion and make a free, rational choice. However, he never coerced a single person to accept Islām against his will. The Muslim scholar **Ibn al-Qayyim** (d. 1350) said: "It will become clear to whoever reflects upon the biographical account of the Prophet (صَلَّى ٱللَّٰهُ عَلَيْهِ وَسَلَّمَ) that he did not compel a single person to accept his religion, ever. Rather, he [only] fought whoever fought against him [first]... the people entered his religion wilfully, out of choice. The majority of the people of the Earth entered his call when guidance became clear to them and that He is the Messenger of God in truth."[99]

There were hundreds of tribes in Arabia. The Prophet only fought hostile tribes and their allies within a specific region of Arabia. At the head of them were his own people, the Quraysh. He fought them because they brought war to him first after they oppressed him, tried to assassinate him multiple times, expelled him and his companions from Mecca, tortured and killed some of his companions, confiscated their homes, property, wealth and

---

[98] *Majmūʿ al-Fatāwā* (19/20).

[99] *Ḥidāyat al-Hayārā* (Dār ʿĀlam al-Fawāʾid) pp. 29-30. They myth of forced conversion by the sword is recognised by non-Muslim historians and writers. **Lawrence Browne** wrote: "Incidentally these well-established facts dispose of the idea so widely fostered in Christian writings that the Muslims, wherever they went, forced people to accept Islam at the point of the sword." *The Prospects of Islām*, London, 1944, p. 12. **James Michener** wrote: "No other religion in history spread so rapidly as Islam. The West has widely believed that this surge of religion was made possible by the sword. But no modern scholar accepts this idea." *Reader's Digest*, May 1955, pp. 68-70. **De Lacy O'Leary** wrote: "History makes it clear, however, that the legend of fanatical Muslims sweeping through the world and forcing Islam at the point of sword upon conquered races is one of the most fantastically absurd myths that historians have ever repeated." *Islam at the Crossroads*, London, 1923.

businesses and also subjected them to a three year socioeconomic boycott that brought them close to death by starvation.

When he successfully repelled their aggression and injustice by sheer right and moral force of truth and justice and came out on top, he showed tremendous mercy to them when he conquered Mecca without battle, through peaceful means alone. He spared its inhabitants—his enemies for 20 years—though he could have killed them all, and told them they are free to go. **Eventually, all of those polytheists became Muslim**. Thereafter, hundreds of delegations travelled to him from all parts of Arabia during the last two years of his life as is well recorded in the history books. These delegations were those of the Jews, Christians and polytheists. Discussions continued to take place about issues of religion **and all of this was *after* the so-called "verses of the sword" were revealed.** This proves that peaceful preaching, discussion and argumentation were never abrogated at all and always remain in effect because they are foundational whereas fighting to repel injustice and hindrance is incidental and due to necessity. The overwhelming majority of these delegations and the tribes they represented accepted Islām, willingly, after being convinced of its truth. Those who declined Islām and chose to remain non-Muslims willingly became citizens under guarantee of protection.

So this explains the purpose of the legislation of this second type of jihād. It is to remove aggression, obstacles and hindrances from peaceful observance, conveyance, discussion and debate. Decisions regarding it are only made by the ruler and the texts pertaining to jihād are addressed to the ruler of the Muslims as has preceded and not to any of the subjects. Further still, any fighting that takes place is only ever against combatants and is prohibited against women, children, the elderly, blind and lame and priests and monks—all of those who have no participation in war. This is also clear proof that the people being fought are not fought just because they are non-Muslims, but because they have engaged in aggression, injustice, hostilities and waging of war.

The above is proof that jihād in Islām has nothing to do with the terrorists who kill non-combatant men, women and children through treachery and perfidy in lands where there is no war, where covenants are clearly in place which they have agreed to by virtue of simply being in the land, **and no one is being hindered from the peaceful practice and proclamation of Islām**.

For this reason, devout orthodox Muslims consider individuals like **Anjem Choudary** and his followers and supporters, groups like **Ḥizb al-Taḥrīr** and **al-Muḥājirūn** to be treacherous and perfidious to God (Allāh), the Most High, and to Islām and its people, before they are treacherous and perfidious to those under whose protection and guarantee of welfare they have chosen to live. There is nothing greater in contradiction to the spirit of Islāmic law, ethics and morals than this. As for the apparent lofty slogans they brandish, it is nothing but beautified, shallow rhetoric.

Likewise, jihād has nothing to do with "*fighting all the infidels until they either convert or are exterminated*" as is alleged by far-right extremists and other Islam haters, a centuries old word of fiction they inherited from those of like hearts and minds who came before them. If their claim was true, Christian priests and Jewish rabbis would be the first to have been killed in every place as a means of totally eliminating their religion and its adherents. And upon that, Jewish Professors like **David J. Wasserstein** would not be writing articles titled, "*How Islām Saved the Jews*"[100] 1400 years later. And nor would Christians have welcomed Muslims to rule over them to escape the tyranny, oppression, slaughter and treachery of their fellow Christians if Islām had a convert or die policy.[101]

The killing of those who are in the churches and synagogues engaged in worship and study is prohibited by Islām as is mentioned by the jurists in the works of Islāmic jurisprudence. The Muslim scholar **Ibn al-Qayyim** (d. 1350) said: "Killing is only necessary in retaliation for war, not in retaliation for unbelief. For this reason, women and children are not killed. Neither are the

---

[100] A 2012 lecture given by Wasserstein and then later published as an article in the Jewish Chronicle, "*So, What Did Islām Do For the Jews*", 24 May 2012.

[101] Refer to the book by the British Orientalist scholar and historian Thomas Walker Arnold, "*The Preaching of Islam*" (London Constable & Company, 1913). Examples from this book were given in a previous chapter to show how Christian populations in numerous lands welcomed Muslims to rule over them because of their justice and fair treatment.

terminally ill and the blind. And neither are the monks who do not fight. Rather, we only fight the one who wages war against us. This was the way of the Prophet (ﷺ) towards the inhabitants of the Earth."[102]

In contrast to the above, the alleged, spurious jihād of the Khārijite extremists discussed in the previous chapter, is against Muslim rulers, governments and societies based upon a revolutionary ideology similar to that of Marxists and Communists. It is based on social, economic and political grievances clothed in religious rhetoric, used to draw in the naive and ignorant as footsoldiers for the cause. The Muslim Brotherhood and al-Qaeda ideology existed well before the illegal and unjust invasions of Afghanistan and Iraq by Western powers, showing that these deviants and extremists were not "created" by foreign policy. Rather, these extremists were already killing Muslim leaders and their subjects from the 1940s onwards on the basis of these extremist ideas they inherited from the Khārijites extremists and terrorists of old.

Western nations have simply come in the way and hindered the goals and plans of the Khārijite extremists. Neoconservative warmongers, corporate terrorists and other propagandists goaded Western governments to make invasions of Afghanistan, Iraq and Syria in order to serve geopolitical ends. In turn the Khārijite extremists have resorted to terrorist acts in the West. These attacks are only spillover activities and are not primarily intended or desired in their ideology. These attacks pale into insignificance when compared to what these extremists do to Muslims because Muslims, their rulers and governments **are their primary targets**.

A 2015 report titled "**The New Jihadism**" which was published by the Department of War Studies at King's College London[103] indicates that during the month of November 2014, chosen as a sample month for the study, a total of 664 attacks led to the deaths of 5042 people, the overwhelming majority of which were in Irāq (1770), Nigeria (786), Afghānistān (782), Syria (693), Yemen (410),

---

[102] *Aḥkām Ahl al-Dhimmah* (1/110).

[103] "*The New Jihadism: A Global Snapshot*", Peter Neumann, International Centre for the Study of Radicalization, Kings College London. p. 14.

Somalia (216) and Pakistan (212). Peter Neumann, the author of the report states: "This report, therefore, tells the story of a movement in the middle of a transformation— one whose final outcome is impossible to predict. The immediate focus, however, is jihadism's human cost: with, on average, more than 20 attacks and nearly 170 deaths per day, jihadist groups destroy countless lives— most of them Muslim— in the name of an ideology that the vast majority of Muslims reject." And he notes in the conclusion: "In just one month, jihadist groups killed 5,042 people—the equivalent of three attacks on the scale of the London bombings in July 2005 each day. Contrary to the often articulated complaint that jihadism is over-reported and that groups like the Islāmic State get too much coverage, our survey seems to suggest that most of the victims receive practically no attention. Hardly any of the attacks that formed the basis for our analysis were reported in the Western media. Indeed, even the suicide bombings— of which there were 38 —made virtually no headlines except in the countries in which they took place. Yet most of the victims of jihadist violence continue to be non-combatants, and the vast majority is Muslim."[104]

As such, all the deceptive, embellished claims of *jihād* made by these insurgents, bandits, revolutionaries and terrorists of al-Qaeda and ISIS are baseless and are only believed by the ignorant and those with deficient intellects, whether Muslims or non-Muslims.

Their actions are nothing but **sedition** and **terrorism** and come under the texts of the Qurʾān and Prophetic traditions that deal with highway-robbery, rebellion, corruption and terrorism all of which have their own treatment within Islāmic law through corporal and capital punishment. The ideology of these people starts with expelling Muslim rulers from Islām on account of perceived injustices. It ends with violence, turmoil, terrorism and destruction of Muslim inhabited lands. This is precisely what al-Qaeda and ISIS have helped to achieve much to the delight of:

- **Ultra-Zionists, Jewish supremacists and extremists** looking to annexe resource rich Syrian and other nearby lands as part of their

---

[104] "*The New Jihadism*", p. 23.

religious, ideological conviction that they have an inherent, race-based right to own and occupy it.[105]

- **Extreme Evangelical Christians** awaiting Armageddon and the destruction of the Arab Muslims so as to hasten the second coming of Christ whom they believe will forcefully convert Jews and Muslims to Christianity by the sword.

- **Neoconservative warmongers and corporate terrorists and vultures** who plan and implement the invasion and destruction of nations for financial, economic and thereby, political gain.

As for Muslims, they gain absolutely nothing from extremist and terrorist groups like ISIS. At least 99.95% of Muslims oppose them and want them destroyed.[106]

In a 2010 interview, **Professor Olivier Roy**[107] was asked the question, "In your book you say that fundamentalist groups like al-Qaeda have nothing to do with Islāmic tradition. But in Europe the fundamentalist ideology is regarded as the essence of the traditional thinking. How do you explain this contradiction?" Within his reply, he noted that, "**Al-Qaeda is not the expression of traditional Islam or even fundamentalist Islam; it is a new understanding of Islam, cloaked in western revolutionary ideology.**"[108]

And short of a decade earlier, **David Forte**, a Professor of Law, wrote just after the September 11 attacks: "Over the past few weeks, I have argued that Osama bin Laden and his Taliban allies represent a perversion of Islam and are engaged in a campaign to change Islām itself to define the faith politically, and not primarily legally or theologically. The evidence, I believe, is unequivocal: His

---

[105] This an undeniable and factually correct statement. These people exist and have well-known statements in this regard which are often freely reported and discussed in Israeli newspapers. These people do not represent nor speak for all Jews and many religious Jews denounce them openly.

[106] Considering that the Muslim population today stands at 1.8 billion people.

[107] He is the Research Director at the French National Center for Scientific Research (CNRS) and lectures at a number of political institutes in Paris. He has numerous books on politics and Islām.

[108] Refer to "*Holy Secularism*" published in *New Perspectives Quarterly*, Wiley Online Library, 20 July 2010.

war is as much against Islam as it is against the West. I have written that Islam is a multivocal religion, that from its start it has debated within itself the nature of its identity. And I have noted that among all its varied traditions, one thing remains clear: The acts of the terrorists of September 11, and the justification of them by Osama bin Laden, replicate in modern guise a violent faction, the Khārijites, that Islām found totally anathema to the faith early in its history. In other writings, I have asserted that this form of extremism has been inspired by the writings of influential modernist radicals, such as Sayyid Quṭb of Egypt, who believe that virtually all Islam is in a state of unbelief and needs to be reconquered. Thus, in its modern form, Bin Laden's kind of extremism has much more in common with Stalin, Hitler, and Mao than it does with Islāmic tradition. Like those state terrorists, Bin Laden is at war with his own people. And finally, I have boldly asserted that bin Laden and his extremists are evil, pure and simple, and Islam is not. Since these opinions have been aired, I have received many letters, telephone calls, and e-mails. Without exception, Muslims who have contacted me have been grateful for my views. They have been relieved to hear how a Christian and Westerner is explaining to Americans the true nature of their religion. They have thanked me for my understanding of Islām. They agree with my characterization of bin Laden and al Qaeda."[109]

Given this, it is unjust for Islām haters and detractors to portray the faulty understanding of the extremists and terrorists as an orthodox reading of Islāmic texts and valid juristic opinion. These criminals have no legal authority for their actions which involve treachery and perfidy.

The late Salafi scholar, **Aḥmad bin Yaḥyā al-Najmī** (d. 2008) said: "The Prophet (صَلَّى ٱللَّٰهُ عَلَيْهِ وَسَلَّمَ) would prohibit perfidy and treachery and he would command truthfulness, innocence and trustworthiness. As for what the terrorists do in this time when they wear bombs or they drive cars loaded with bombs and on finding a gathering of people they blow up themselves or blow up just the car, then this

[109] "Religion is not the enemy", The National Review, 19th October 2001.

practice is built upon deception, Islām is far, far away from this and does not affirm it at all. What is being done now of suicide missions in Britain or other lands, they are planned and executed by the Takfīrī Khārijites, These people are from the organisation of al-Qaeda, those who follow Usāmah bin Lādin, [Muḥammad] al-Misʿarī and Saʿd al-Faqīh and their likes who have been nurtured upon the books of thinkers such as Sayyid Quṭb."[110]

The late Salafi scholar, **Shaykh Zayd ibn Muḥammad al-Madkhalī** (d. 2014) was asked: "There are some people who say that bombings in the non-Muslim lands are valid in return for what they do of butchering Muslims in Palestine and elsewhere. What is the foundation regarding this issue?" He responded:

"Such people are merely speaking with their own opinions without any semblance of Islāmic knowledge supporting it. This because there are covenants and agreements between nation states. Every state has (agreements) of security with its neighbours. Hence, treachery is not permitted at all and this is not from the legislated jihād, rather it is from amongst the prohibited crimes because of what results from it of harm. This transgression is not correct even if it was against a non-Muslim, it is not correct ever. There is no evidence supporting it at all. Rather, there are agreements and covenants between the various states. Thus, it is not permissible for anyone to traverse the path of chaos, such that chaos spreads throughout the world, the affairs are overturned and harm comes to Muslims, non-Muslims, the innocent from humanity and those whose blood Islām has made inviolable. These bombings, assassinations and suicide missions are Satanic improvisations for which no evidence is established from the Book and the Prophetic traditions. Rather, they are only in accordance with erroneous understandings in which their proponents have erred. They will bear their own burdens alongside the burdens of all those whom they misguided from those they have enlisted as soldiers and who have obeyed and followed them without evidence. They have convinced them that they are engaged in

---

[110] In a dictated statement titled, "*The Sunnah is Innocent of Terrorist Activities*" and issued on 26 August 2005, a short while after the 2005 London 7/7 attacks.

jihād in the path of Allāh but they have lied regarding that. The true jihād is the one in which its conditions are met and its preventative barriers are absent. Have these misguided sects followed the path of true jihād? The answer is no.... They have no authority except following desires and obeying Satan. They did whatever they did of shedding blood and destroying property out of envious jealousy, transgression and oppression. Thus, they deserve the [capital] punishments due to the people of corruption and crime."[111] End of quote.

These condemnations are unequivocal and clear. There is no single text in the Qur'ān or the Prophetic traditions or any juristic opinion from the traditional schools of law in Islām that encourages or justifies the killing of non-combatants in remote lands such as what is done today in Europe and North America of acts of terrorism. Rather, Islām emphatically prohibits killing non-combatants even during war itself. Islām demands the fulfilment of all contracts, agreements and covenants in host countries and condemns treachery and perfidy. It is forbidden for Muslims to cause public nuisance and agitation in non-Muslim lands, let alone harm or even kill people. Marches and demonstrations do not have any basis in Islāmic texts. Rather, they have been imported into Islām from Marxist and Communist revolutionary ideology and are employed by extreme sects like the Muslim Brotherhood to foment revolutions and topple authorities as a means of snatching power.

All people of sound mind know that the acts of sinful Muslims who engage in terrorism—[as well as organised crime including theft, drug-dealing, rape, prostitution and the likes] all of which are condemned in Islām and for which corporal and capital punishments exist—cannot be ascribed to Islām from near or afar.

To do so would be the same as arguing that Islām enourages the consumption of alcohol merely because Muslims can be found who habitually engage in it. This is clear dishonesty and is the way of far-right nationalist movements who try to ascribe the crimes of sinful, ignorant Muslims to Islām to serve their own agendas.

---

[111] Refer to *Nuzhāt al-Qārī Fī Sharḥ Kitāb al-ʿIlm Min Ṣaḥīḥ al-Bukhārī* (102-103).

The extremists and terrorists clothe and beautify their terrorism as jihād. They claim that the verses relating to fighting and war—which are addressed only to the rulers of the Muslims—have abrogated the verses of peaceful preaching, discussion and argumentation. This is a blatantly dishonest, false and refuted view whose invalidation is clear from what has preceded.

In summary, there are two groups who attempt to present their fallacious understanding of Islām as mainstream Islām:

- Those Muslims who have adopted extremist ideologies which have no basis in mainstream orthodox Islām but only in the deviant ideologies of the Khārijite extremists. They seek to achieve their goals by legitimising their actions with interpretations that are novel and false.
- Those non-Muslims—both secular and religious—who have prior ideological hatred of Islām and delight in the existence of these extremists because of the utility they provide in a) scaring people away from Islām, b) winning converts to their faith or cause and c) furthering their racial, national or geopolitical agendas.

Both of these groups are two sides of the same coin and have the same twisted view of Islām. Hence, both are active recruiters and aiders and abetters of the terrorists by their propagation of this false understanding of Islām and treating it to be the Islām of the Prophet (صَلَّى ٱللَّهُ عَلَيْهِ وَسَلَّمَ), his Companions and of orthodox Muslims.

After the clarification regarding extremist and terrorism, we move on to discuss the issue of women, which is also used to engineer a large amount of negative press about Islām.

Islām and Women

With sustained media coverage of Muslims in the context of global conflicts, more and more people continue to show interest in Islām and its teachings. Access to unbiased sources of information about Islām has been made easy through the Internet as well as increased interactions between Muslims and non-Muslims.

The trend in conversions continues to grow and **the majority of converts are women** who outnumber male converts with **a ratio of four to one.**[112] This is despite extremely negative media coverage in light of acts of terrorism and claims that Islām denigrates women.

Converts are typically well-educated, tend to be in professional occupations, come from a variety of backgrounds and comprise Christians, Jews, Atheists, Hindūs, Sikhs and others. This reveals that inquisitive rational, thinking people who are fair-minded and are willing to look beyond the propaganda are finding **intellectual and spiritual satisfaction** which materialist societies and other religions have been unable to offer them.

What is attracting these women to Islām?

Many are disillusioned with Christianity and its confusing theology that a critical mind is unable to decipher. Mysterious doctrines do not offer satisfactory answers about divinity. Many of these women converts state that they find a clear and intelligible treatment of divinity in Islām. Others discover—with plenty of research and reflection—the great honour that Islām confers upon women, contrary to the propaganda in the media and the claims of detractors. Others find stability in their lives due to the moral certitude provided by Islāmic teachings compared to hazy, contradictory and shallow notions of morals in other philosophies and religions. Many see that women are objectified and exploited in Western societies and come to the realisation that slogans such as "*women's rights*", "*women's equality*" and "*women's freedom*" are shallow, meaningless and hypocritical, especially when sales of goods depend upon naked women and prostitution is made a taxable occupation as is the case in some European nations. Others

---

[112] As reported in "*Women and Conversion to Islām: The American Women's Experience*" by Elkoubaiti Naoualv, 2010.

have found an antidote in Islām to a particular mind virus which infects women, causes them to both mimic and hate men at the same time, and causes them to metamorphosise into hate-filled spiteful monsters far removed from their true feminine nature. The reasons are many and diverse and cannot all be enumerated. Secularists, atheists, feminists and many other groups are both grieved and baffled by this phenomenon.[113]

What is observed today in Western secular liberal nations is the orchestrated destruction of the family unit by the erosion of masculinity for biological males and femininity for biological females through the promotion of sexual liberation philosophies, emasculation and feminisation of men, instilling distrust and hatred of men in the name of "feminism"[114] and "equality",

---

[113] Secular, socialist, liberal societies exploit women primarily for **commercial objectives** and to advance collectivist agendas that require the family unit and traditional values to be eroded. The woman is not given any unique, special rights in such societies but is manipulated through social engineering into roles and behaviours that have little to do with genuine liberation of women and keeping her true to her nature. Rather, they have more to do with eroding the family institution—which is the basis of inheritance and private property rights—and exploiting women as an **under-tapped labour force** to expand the reach of taxable economies. Such economies must service the debt imposed upon them through privately owned banking institutions that create money as debt and charge interest upon it. This is the true and real reason why women have been encouraged to leave the home and enter the workplace in the name of liberation and equality. It is primarily to double the taxable workforce to help service the national debt. In addition, women are considered huge markets ready to be exploited for profit at the expense of their personal and private interests which include health, modesty and chastity. This is aided by promoting liberal philosophies and lifestyles. Many Western women become worn out, disillusioned, feel out of touch with their inner selves and yearn for something that will give true meaning, purpose and satisfaction to their lives. This is the reason why many women are accepting Islām, because its guidance is based on justice and on the fundamental facts and realities of human nature.

[114] Feminism is anti-women because it encourages women to reject, despise and abandon their femininity and adopt masculinity by mimicking what men do in order to prove to men that they can also be masculine and are therefore equal to them. This is a very twisted form of psychology that leads to twisted individuals and personalities. The failure of mainstream feminism is well known and much research exists regarding it. Abandoning your true

destroying the institution of marriage and promoting gender confusion and sexual indoctrination in children which is really a form of horrendous child abuse.[115] Muslims, and in fact even many non-Muslims, reject the notion that 20th century capitalist, hedonist, narcissistic Western culture is the universal model against which all other cultures or values are evaluated. Thus, the status, rights and obligations of women in Islām are to be understood within the wider social and legal framework of Islām itself and the aims of such a framework. From these aims are keeping men and women true to their natures, protecting their beneficial interests, and cementing family ties so that strong, stable societies are produced. It cannot be evaluated by materialist, hedonistic, narcissistic and liberal philosophies.

ca

The woman plays a central and crucial role in the family, society and nation as a mother. Because the family unit is of the utmost importance in Islām, the Muslim woman has been given multiple layers of protection through a specific social and economic structure along with a wide range of guaranteed rights that make it difficult to harass and exploit her in a society that faithfully abides by Islām and honours her status.[116]

---

nature and pretending to be something you are not is self-delusion and self-subjugation, not liberation.

[115] Refer to the excellent article, "*Gender Ideology Harms Children*" published by the American College of Pediatricians on https://www.acpeds.org and also "*Transgender is 'Mental Disorder;' Sex Change 'Biologically Impossible'*" by Michael Chapman on https://cnsnews.com, 2 June 2015. Refer also to Dr. Judith Weisman's book "*Kinsey, Sex and Fraud*" (1993) and her informative website: http://www.drjudithreisman.com. Alfred Kinsey—*absurdly celebrated as a hero*—was a sex-researcher who, from a distance, oversaw the sexual abuse and molestation of babies and infants as part of his research to promote sexual freedom and the exercise of lust between all ages without restraint. **His ideas form the foundation of all modern sex education in schools** which is essentially to use the cover of providing safe-sex instructions to children whilst advancing Kinsey's agenda of early sexualizuation.

[116] In Western nations, the woman is only treated as an equal to man after she has been **stripped of her feminine qualities** and **denied her rights**, such as the

As for that which takes place in Muslim countries of oppression, withholding rights from women or denying women opportunities which Islām allows them, then all of that returns to local cultural influences and traditions.

Men and women are equal in the sight of God and differ only in a limited number of injunctions that return back to established physical and biological differences between them. Women have been given numerous concessions not afforded to men on account of such differences. Aside from these differences, men and women are equal in terms of their **origins**, their **status and worth** in the sight of God, their **religious duties**, their **reward**s and their **material rights**.

In terms of **origins**, men and women are considered equal in that they were created from a single soul:

خَلَقَكُم مِّن نَّفْسٍ وَٰحِدَةٍ ثُمَّ جَعَلَ مِنْهَا زَوْجَهَا

"**He created you from one soul, then He made from it its mate.**" (39:6).

The woman was not created from any components besides those from which man was created. All of humanity were created and spread through a single male and single female.[117] Likewise, men are of women and women are of men[118] in the sense that they are begotten of each other. As such, the male and female are twin halves to each other, as we see in the Prophetic tradition, "*Women are the twin-halves of men.*"[119]

In terms of **status** and **rewards**, men and women are considered equal in that their righteous deeds are given the exact same weight and recompense in the hereafter, as indicated in many texts.[120]

In terms of **religious duties**, men and women are equally bound by Islām's pillars and obligations since they are addressed in the Qur'ān collectively as "*O you who believe*" and separately through

---

legal right to be provided for without being forced to work or spend out of her own wealth.

[117] Refer to Qur'ān (4:1).

[118] Refer to Qur'ān (3:195).

[119] Related by Muslim (no. 635), Aḥmad in al-Musnad (6/256) and others.

[120] Refer to the Qur'ān (4:124), (33:35), by way of example.

the terms "*believing men*" (muʾminūn) and "*believing women*" (muʾmināt).[121] They are also equal in terms of legal injunctions and procedures that pertain to rights, obligations and criminal acts in which life, property, honour are violated.

As for **material rights**, the Prophet (ﷺ) granted Muslim women the rights of:

- **education, ownership, property, inheritance shares**
- **buying, selling, contracting, renting, lending, mortgaging**
- **sponsoring, guaranteeing, suing, freedom of expression**
- **and keeping her family name** among others.

Most of these rights were not available to European women until the 19th and 20th centuries. They were only granted to them with much reluctance and resentment on behalf of men, and in many cases, after lengthy campaigns and violence.

No nation in history gave this degree of freedom and equality to women prior to Islām and after it, even until recent times.

As for the affairs in which men and women are treated differently, then that returns back to the fundamental facts of human nature in that men and women differ in some respects. The woman has both strengths and weaknesses that the man does not have and vice versa, the man has strengths and weaknesses that the woman does not have. These differences do not mean that one is superior to the other, since superiority in the sight of God only has one factor and that is piety:

إِنَّ أَكْرَمَكُمْ عِندَ ٱللَّهِ أَتْقَىٰكُمْ

"**Indeed, the most noble of you in the sight of God (Allāh) is the most pious of you.**" (49:13).

The strengths of the man are a cover for the woman and the strengths of the woman are a cover for the man. So in Islām, a man and a woman are a **complimentary pair** that make a unit, like lock and key. Islām enjoins and inculcates those affairs that cement this relationship **on grounds of justice**, which is to put everything in its proper place, and not on imaginary grounds of absolute equality, since men and women are not equal in all respects. Differences between men and women are firmly established in **biological**,

[121] Refer to the Qurʾān (9:72).

psychological, brain and **military** studies and are undeniable.[122] On account of these fundamental facts of human nature, men have been given a degree over women in the sense that their physical and biological constitution makes them more suited for having the responsibility of maintenance, provision and protection. For this reason, they are referred to in the Qurʾān as "qawwāmūn", the maintainers and protectors of women, because of this extra degree and because they spend upon women. As the Qurʾānic exegetes explain, this extra degree does not mean in rank and status, but in ability and responsibility. This is because rank and status do not lie in physical and biological constitution, but in faith and piety.[123]

Once the above is clear, we may address a number of issues that are frequently raised about women in Islām in order to make it appear that she is oppressed.

1. The Ḥijāb and the Niqāb

The topic of hijāb is quite easy to understand in light of the phenomena of sexual harrasment in Western secular, liberal nations. In August 2016 media outlets in the UK ran headlines covering a Trade Union Congress survey which indicated that **sexual harassment of women has reached "shocking" levels and that between half to two-thirds of women experience sexual advancements or harassment by males at work in relation to their bodies or clothes.**[124]

---

[122] Refer to the excellent February 2015 paper by the Center for Military Readiness titled, "*New British Ministry of Defence Review Paper Shreds Case for Women in Ground Close Combat (GCC)*" which summarises a report by the Ministry of Defence (MoD). The report presents key physical, biological and mental differences between men and women and is a very interesting read.

[123] Shaykh Maḥmūd Shākir, commenting on Imām al-Ṭabarī's report from Ibn ʿAbbās (رَضِيَ ٱللَّهُ عَنْهُ) in this subject, stated about the Qurʾānic verse that refers to men as "qawwāmūn": "It is not informing about any [inherent] excellence Allāh has decreed for the man regardless of whether he behaves righteously in what He commanded him or behaves sinfully." *Tafsīr al-Ṭabarī* (Cairo, 2nd edition) 4/536-537.

[124] See "*Half of women 'sexually harassed at work' - TUC survey*" BBC News, 16 August 2016; "*Sexual harassment at work is getting worse. We need to stamp it out*" The Guardian, 10 August 2016; "*Workplace sexual harassment at 'shocking' level*"

The hijāb is one of numerous elements within Islāmic guidance that work together in a complimentary fashion to: a) protect and maintain women's personal respect, dignity and honour b) free women from the tyranny of having to please male onlookers and meet standards of beauty dictated by exploiters and profiteers, as well as the tyranny of the belief that their worth is proportional to their sexual charms, and from the tyranny of all the physical, emotional and material costs associated with all of the above and c) foster an environment in which women interact and conduct their affairs free of harassment and of unwanted sexual advances.

In light of the above, the following points in explanation of the ḥijāb will suffice:

First: Muslim women view Mary (عَلَيْهَاٱلسَّلَامُ), the Mother of Jesus (عَلَيْهِٱلسَّلَامُ), as a symbol of purity, modesty and chastity. Mary was an extremely devout woman who was favoured by God (Allāh) over all other women. She is described in the Qur'ān as a purified, chaste woman who was true in intention, word and deed. Muslim women proudly and unashamedly take Mary (عَلَيْهَاٱلسَّلَامُ) as their role-model and view her praiseworthy qualities as essential elements of a woman's respectability, dignity and honour.[125]

ITV.Com, 10 August 2016. Much of this harrassment involves comments of a sexual nature about the body or clothes. As for research, then the following are some resources: Koukounas E, Letch NM. *Psychological correlates of perception of sexual intent in women.* J Soc Psychol. 2001 Aug;141(4):443-56; Awasthi B. From *Attire to Assault: Clothing, Objectification, and De-humanization—A Possible Prelude to Sexual Violence?* Front Psychol. 2017 Mar 10;8:338; Mclaughlin K, Harnish RJ. *The Effects of Clothing and Dyad Sex Composition on Perceptions of Sexual Intent: Do Women and Men Evaluate These Cues Differently.* Journal of Applied Social Psychology, 1987,17,2, pp. 108-126. Guéguen N. *The effect of women's suggestive clothing on men's behavior and judgment: a field study.* Psychol Rep. 2011 Oct;109(2):635-8; Nicolas Guéguen, Jordy Stefan. *Men's Judgment and Behavior Toward Women Wearing High Heels.* Journal of Human Behavior in the Social Environment Vol. 25 , Iss. 5, 2015.

[125] Next time you see a Muslim woman dressed in hijāb, do not look at her through the subjective spectacles of the Islām haters and rabid, hate-filled, psychologically twisted feminists but through her own eyes: A woman who seeks to please God by emulating the qualities of Mary, the mother of Jesus—[who was very devout and protective of her modesty and chastity]—and a woman who seeks ownership and control of her own sexuality, by wrestling it back from male exploiters and profiteers.

Second: The Qurʾān orders Muslim women to draw their outer garments (jilbāb) over their bodies, describing it as being better for them in that they are known as respectable women and not harassed or harmed (33:59). It commands women to be modest and protect their chastity by not engaging in illicit sexual acts and not to show off their beauty and adornment except what is naturally apparent thereof. Likewise, to draw the khimār (covering) over their heads, necks and chests and not to display their beauty except to their husbands, fathers, sons, fathers-in-law, step-sons, brothers, nephews, other women, the old who lack vigour and young male children who are not yet aware of the private affairs of women (24:31). On the basis of these texts and Prophetic traditions Muslim scholars have mentioned numerous conditions and descriptions of a Muslim woman's hijāb that fulfil and serve the objectives intended behind it.

Third: Female converts find within Islām and within the hijāb a reclamation of their femininity. They recognise it as an antidote to the degradation caused by immodesty, immorality and sexual permissiveness. These affairs are glorified by lifestyle philosophies cleverly presented as freedom and liberation of women but which are really aimed at social engineering and benefiting profiteers. These profiteers make billions in various industries by exploiting the nature of women psychologically and physically as a means of influencing the economic activities of both men and women.

Hijāb puts an end to unwarranted oppression and exploitation, which is why there is so much propaganda against it and why Muslim women who wear it are wrongly described as "oppressed" and "subjugated". Rather, Muslim women consider themselves empowered and liberated by it.

As for the niqāb, which is the veil, then this is not obligatory in Islām. However, a small number of women choose to wear the veil purely out of devotion to God, and not because they support al-Qaeda or ISIS. These women seek to please God and to emulate the modesty and chastity of Mary (عَلَيْهَا ٱلسَّلَامُ), who isolated herself from males and devoted herself to God. Christian nuns are seen as symbols of modesty, chastity and religious devotion due to their wilfully chosen isolation in convents and monasteries away from the public sphere. Women who wear the niqāb like to be seen in the same way except that they do not participate in organised physical isolation in places of worship.

2. Females only receive half the inheritance of males

This would only be a valid doubt if males and females had *equal financial obligations.* In Islāmic law, females are absolved of all financial obligations. It is obligatory upon the man to provide shelter, food, clothing and that by which a woman maintains her hygiene and beauty according to what is customary. Further, the woman has control over her own financial affairs and all of her personal wealth and property—whether through inheritance, gifting or business—is entirely her own. She is not obliged to spend out of her wealth on the basic needs mentioned earlier.

The late scholar, **Shaykh Ibn al-'Uthaymīn** (d. 2001) stated: "It is obligatory upon a man to spend on his family, upon his wife and children with what is customary. Even if his wife was rich, it is still obligatory upon the husband to spend. And in relation to this, if the wife teaches, having specified this as a condition of marriage upon the husband, that he enables her to teach, then he has no right to take anything from her salary, not even half of it, nor less than or greater than it."[126] Upon this, due to the greater financial burden upon the man, his share is twice that of a woman. Men have to spend not only on their wives and children, but also on their parents, sisters and younger male siblings. Hence, it is perfect justice for the man to receive twice the share of a woman **on the basis of responsibility**. If the woman was treated equally and given the same share, without an equal burden of responsibility, it would be injustice against the man.

It is important to understand the difference between **justice**—which means putting everything in its proper place—and abstract notions of equality. Treating people with equality in situations where they should be treated with justice, is actually injustice, inequality and corruption.

In Islāmic law—in accordance with the fundamental facts and realities of human nature—it is not in the beneficial interests of

---

[126] Refer to his *Sharḥ Riyāḍ al-Ṣāliḥīn* (6/143).

children, the husband, the family unit, the society and the whole nation for women to be burdened with working to support themselves and their children. This does not mean they are prohibited to work, since societies need qualified and competent women in numerous fields such as teaching, medicine and the likes. However, it does not place an equal burden on women to work in order to provide for themselves and their children. Rather, the foundation is that they are free of all responsibilities in this regard, while being permitted to work, according to need, in fields and occupations that benefit to the society. Hence, the disparity in inheritance shares—which are based on factual ground realities and not just upon abstract notions of equality—and this is the essence of justice.

Alongside the above, it is not always the case that the female receives half the share of the male. A detailed study of inheritance laws in Islām, makes clear that this only takes place in **four scenarios** out of around **at least thirty-five possible scenarios**. In other scenarios the female takes an equal or greater share than the male and in somes instances she takes a share when the male does not receive any at all.

3. A woman's testimony "is equal to half of man's"

This doubt involves misrepresentation of a verse in the Qur'ān that provides guidelines for loan transactions. It is a very specific scenario in which the lender is advised to have the contract put into writing, with the borrower or his guardian dictating the terms of the loan to a scribe. The verse further advises that two men are brought to act as witnesses, and "**if two men are not available then a man and two women, from those that you are pleased with as witnesses**" (2:282). From here, it is argued that Islām denigrates women because it reduces their testimony to half that of a man, thereby making her equal to half a man in worth and status.

To answer this doubt, a broad observation is made first followed by more specific points. As for the broad observation:

The truth value of testimony in Islām is independent of gender and is based upon **integrity (ʿādālah)** and **precision (ḍabṭ)**. One should keep in mind that one of the greatest scholars in Islām was

ʿĀʾishah (رَضِيَ اللَّهُ عَنْهَا), the wife of the Prophet (صَلَّى اللَّهُ عَلَيْهِ وَسَلَّمَ). She was also a jurist[127] and transmitter of the Prophetic traditions. Many women were known for interpreting law, giving legal rulings (fatwā) and transmitting the Prophetic traditions. The Wives of the Prophet (صَلَّى اللَّهُ عَلَيْهِ وَسَلَّمَ) were ordered to memorise and convey what they had been taught of the Qurʾān and legal injunctions. Hence, they feature prominently among those who interpreted law and gave legal verdicts.[128] They include: ʿĀʾishah, Umm Salamah, Ṣafiyyah, Ḥafṣah, Umm Ḥabībah, Juwayriyah and Maymūnah (رَضِيَ اللَّهُ عَنْهُنَّ). Thereafter, Umm al-Dardāʾ, Nuṣaybah bint al-Ḥārith, Laylā bint Qāʾif, Asmā bint Abī Bakr, Umm Sharīk, Fāṭimah, Umm Ayman, Umm Yūsuf, are among others that were listed by the scholar, Ibn al-Qayyim for giving legal rulings.[129] As **interpreting law**, **issuing legal rulings** (fatwa) and **transmitting reports** (riwāyah) involve intellectual capacity and an element of testimony, then the verse in question must have **some other consideration** behind the need for corroboration of a woman's act of witnessing in the realm of loan contracts. Muslim scholars discussed this matter and provided a number of explanations. From them were Ibn Taymiyyah (d. 1328) and Ibn al-Qayyim (d. 1350) who both rejected the claim of the universal application of the *two women equal one man* rule in a court of law with clear evidences.

This general observation can then be detailed and explained further through the specific points of clarification:

First: The scenario described in the verse relates to **private contractual affairs relating to loans** in which the parties involved are advised to protect their interests and rights from future challenge through a written contract witnessed by those whom they are pleased with as witnesses. **This has no connection to the act of giving testimony in a court of law.** The scholar and jurist, Ibn al—Qayyim (d. 1350) wrote about this verse: "This is a command to the people of rights [to take such measures with] which they are

---

[127] The 14th century scholar **al-Zarkashi** authored a work, "*Al-Iṣābah fīmā Istadrakahu ʿĀʾishah ʿalā al-Ṣaḥābah*" in which he listed all the affairs in which ʿĀʾishah challenged the legal opinions of the Companions of the Prophet.

[128] Refer to the Qurʾān (33:34).

[129] Refer to *Iʿlām al-Muwaqqiʿīn* (Dār Ibn al-Jawzī) 1/18-22.

able to protect their rights."[130] And Ibn Taymiyyah (d. 1328) explained that this verse does not mention the two categories of two men and one man and two women **as routes of judgement in a court of law** but only as means through which a private individual may protect his right from future challenge. After mentioning and summarising the verse, he said: "All of this is advice, teaching and instruction for them—[the parties engaged in loan contracts]—regarding that by which they may safeguard their rights [from future challenge]. That by which [personal] rights are safeguarded is one thing and that by which judgement is made by a judge [in a court of law] is another thing."[131] Ibn al-Qayyim also states: "There is nothing in the Qur'ān which requires that judgements are not made except through two male witnesses or a male and two female witnesses. For Allāh, the Sublime, only gave this command to the people with rights [in loan contracts], so that they may protect their rights through this particular level of evidence. But He did not command the judges [in courts of law] to judge with this, let alone command them to judge by this alone [in all disputes]. For this reason, the judge may pass judgement by way of breaches [of contract], refusal to take oath, the [testimony] of a single woman, and of individual women with no man present with them..."[132]

Second: In reiteration of the above, this verse is speaking about the **act of witnessing or mental recording** in private loan contracts and not the **act of giving testimony** in a court of law. These are two separate issues and the origin of the doubt comes from confusing between these two affairs.

Third: As for giving testimony in a court of law, there are other situations covered in Islāmic law in which the woman's testimony stands on its own right and is equal to that of a man, such as when she is accused by her husband of adultery and who is unable to bring witnesses. Her testimony **on its own** is sufficient to repel his allegation. In some situations her testimony is given precedence to that of a man, such as in those areas which are specialities and private affairs of women.

---

[130] *Al-Ṭuruq al-Ḥukmiyyah* of Ibn al-Qayyim (Dār ʿAlam al-Fawāʾid) p. 396.
[131] Ibid. p. 183.
[132] Ibid. p. 359.

Fourth: The Muslim scholars have given two explanations as to why, if two men are not available, a man and two women are recommended to act as witnesses in the loan contract.

The first explanation is that **the ability of some women** to commit details to memory may be affected by the various states they pass through due to their nature. Women undergo significant changes which have the capacity to affect mental performance to a degree that can impact the rights of others. "Women go through significant biological changes across their lifespan, more so than men, so these cyclic shifts can disrupt, malfunction, or create disease."[133] These include **menstruation, pregnancy, the postnatal period, breast-feeding** and **menopause** in which hormonal fluxes take place. For this reason—according to this explanation—two women and one man are advised if two men are not available to witness the contract. Hence, the Qur'ān stated, "**if one of them errs**" and not "**when one of them errs**" proving that this does not apply to all women, and not all the time. Rather, this guideline is a safeguarding mechanism in the circumstances of the transaction which the lender is advised to adopt in order to protect his right in the case of future challenge.

The second explanation is that such affairs are not routinely and habitually entered into by women because of the different economic roles of men and women—given that in Islām, women are relieved of all financial responsibilities in providing for the family, this being the responsibility of men. Therefore, both men and women are prone to forgetting things that are not part of their daily experience. As such, the verse explains in this regard, "**so that if one of them errs, then one of them can remind the other..**" (2:82). The scholar and jurist Ibn Taymiyyah (d. 1328) said: "This is so that one of them can remind the other if she errs. This takes place with respect to affairs in which erring is habitual due to forgetfulness and absence of precision..."[134] He is alluding to the fact that due to the absence of familiarity with financial terms and

---

[133] Deborah Serani, PhD, Associate Professor at the Derner Institute of Advanced Psychology Studies as cited in "*4 Mental Health Issues That Are More Common In Women*" on Prevention.Com, 2 September 2016.

[134] Ibid. pp. 399-400.

expertise and experience in these affairs, a person may be prone to forgetfulness and lack precision in recollection. However, as for affairs in which the woman is not prone to error—because she is informed and experienced in them—then her testimony is not equal to half a man's testimony. Ibn Taymiyyah stated: "As for testimony in [fields] in which there is no fear of habitual error, then she is not equal, in such testimony, to half a man."[135] This means that when any person—*male or female*—has knowledge and expertise in a field, then the capacity for error is reduced.

Fifth: Supporting this is what has been stated by Ibn al-Qayyim: "There is no doubt that the wisdom in having plurality [of women in this verse regarding loan contracts] is only with respect to recording the testimony (al-taḥammul). As for when the woman is intelligent and is trustworthy in religion, then her report [in giving testimony] suffices in attaining the objective, just as it does in the field of transmitting reports regarding religious affairs. For this reason, her individual testimony is accepted in numerous situations." And then he cites from Ibn Taymiyyah: "Two women have been put in the place of a man only in the act of witnessing, to observe and record in memory (al-taḥammul), so that one of them does not later forget. This is different to giving testimony (al-ʿadāʾ) [from what has been recorded in memory].[136] **For there is nothing in the Book nor the Sunnah which requires that judgement [in a court of law] cannot be made except with the testimony of two women [in place of a man].** And the command to get two women to act as witnesses to observe [the details at the time of the contract] does not make it binding that judgement [in a court of law] cannot be made with less than two [women]. " Then Ibn al-Qayyim states: "Thus, the routes by which a judge makes judgement [in a court of law] are broader than the routes through which a person safeguards his right." [137]

Sixth: The conditions stated in this verse are specific to loan contracts, not business transactions in general or testimonies in a court of law. Women are free to buy and sell and engage in trade

---

[135] Ibid. p. 400.

[136] Meaning, in providing the details of what she witnessed.

[137] *Iʿlām al-Muwaqqiʿīn* (Dār Kutub al-ʿIlmiyyah) 1/75.

and business—alongside what this entails of making contracts—without requiring two women to conduct business with a single male. This would be necessitated if the claim of the detractors of Islām was true, and this only exposes their stupidity, shallowness and ignorance.

Seventh: As for **testimony** in a court of law in which a judgement is made in relation to people's rights including life, wealth, property and personal honour and establishing justice, then being male or female is not a criterion of truthfulness. Rather, the criteria of acceptance as a witness are **integrity (ʿadālah)** and **precision (ḍabṭ)**. Further, in a court of law, the **evidence (bayyinah)** must be established by the judge, and the nature and form of this evidence is much broader and wider. As such, Islāmic law makes distinctions between three affairs:

a) being called to act as a witness (**ish-hād**)
b) giving testimony (**shahādah**) which is recollection, and
c) establishing evidence (**bayyinah**) to decide a case

Evidence used to decide a case in a court of law is established through a large number of routes and it can be anything by which truth is established. It is not hinged in any way to the guidance given to individuals in private loan contracts, as has been clarified and explained by both Ibn Taymiyyah and Ibn al-Qayyim.

In summary of the above, there is nothing in this verse which renders women equal to half of men in worth and status and nor anything which makes them of *general intellectual inferiority*. Rather, because women go through significant biological changes across their lifespan, more so than men, they are more prone to cognitive impairment during those changes, **and in some women, not all**, it can be to a degree that could affect the rights of others. For that reason, in the realm of private loan contracts, individuals are advised to safeguard their rights by having two women mentally record the details of the contract so that in the case of future challenge, if one of them errs in recollection, the other can remind her. The deficiency of women is restricted to this affair alone and does not imply *general intellectual inferiority*. For this reason the scholar and jurist **Shaykh ʿAbd al-ʿAzīz bin Bāz** (d. 1999) gave caution in this matter by stating: "**This does not necessitate that**

she is deficient in everything, not from the angle of her piety towards God (Allāh), nor from the angle of her establishing His command and nor from the angle of her precision in the affairs she enters into... Thus, it is not befitting for a believer to accuse her of deficiency in every affair."[138] He further added that there are many women who excel over a great number of men in terms of intellect, precision and religiosity, which is most certainly true.

As for witnesses giving testimony in a court of law, then no school of law in Islām has restricted a judge to using only two male witnesses or in their absence, one male and two female witnesses. Rather, admissibility of evidence in a court of law is based on credibility and precision and not determined by gender in the case of testimony (shahādah), which is only one route of many by which evidence is established.

4. Female circumcision

This is a popular misconception spread through the phrase *female genital mutiliation* (FGM) which is frequently and deceptively linked with Islām when it is in fact a sub-Saharan African practice that predated Islām and took on a cultural dimension. The ancient Egyptians practiced what is known as *pharoanic circumcision*, a harmful procedure which damages the female genitals. This spread to sub-Saharan Africa after the Egyptians conquered those lands. Further, Ethiopia and Eritrea are **Christian majority countries** in which around 80% of females on average undergo circumcision today.[139] Females of many other African countries are circumcised, irrespective of their religion and outside Africa, female circumsion is not common in Muslim countries. To connect female genital mutilation with Islām is clear deception and is another tool in the arsenal of Islām haters and rabid, twisted, spiteful feminists.

In order to clarify this issue:

First: There are three types of circumcision procedures:

- **Clitoral unhooding** or **clitoral hood reduction**. This is the removal of a part of the layer of skin covering the clitoris, also

---

[138] Refer to *Majmuʿ Fatāwā wa Maqālāt* (4/292).

[139] Refer to the World Health Organization's website at http://www.who.int under "Female Genital Mutiliation".

known as the clitoral prepuce. It is a fold of skin that is equivalent to the male foreskin. This is a beneficial procedure for women with clear benefits that are documented in the scientific literature.

- **Excision**, also known as "**clitoridectomy**". This is the removal of all or part of the clitoris.

- **Infibulation**, also known as "**pharoanic circumcision**". This is where the external parts of the female genitalia, as well as the labia minora and the clitoris are removed and then the vagina is stitched together. This is **a barbaric practice** and **a crime against women.** This action predated Islām and unfortunately, remained a cultural practice in some African lands.

Second: The size and shape of the prepuce, or the clitoral hood, varies among females, just as the foreskin does in men. As a result, some women may suffer from any of the following: **sexual health problems including unsightly appearance and lack of stimulation, urinary tract and yeast infections, adhesion which is known medically as phimosis,**[140] **sexual pain, and irritation**. There are surgeries spread all across the United States that specialise in this procedure of "hoodplasty", or "clitoral hood reduction" in order to treat these conditions. This procedure is *commended* (and *not* obligatory) for women in Islāmic law and is known as "*al-khitān*", circumcision for women.

Third: In Madīnah, the Prophet (ﷺ) came across a woman that would perform female circumcision from prior to Islām and he advised her: "*Do not cut in excess and thereby cause harm...*"—and in a narration, "*make only a small cut*"—"*... for it brings the woman greater attention [from her husband]*"—and in a narration, "*...for it brings radiance to the face*"—"*and it is more loved by the husband.*"[141] Upon this, Muslim scholars and jurists have made it clear that it is the prepuce (qulfah), the fold of skin comprising the hood that covers

---

[140] See Alei, G. et al. *New Approach to Clitoral Phimosis: Hoodplasty*. Journal of Gynecologic Surgery. Vol. 27, No. 1, March 2011. Research indicates that one in 5 women experience this. Refer to: Munarriz, R. et al. (2002) *The Prevalence of Phimosis of the Clitoris in Women Presenting to the Sexual Dysfunction Clinic*. Journal of Sex & Marital Therapy Vol. 28; Aerts, L. et al. (2017). *The prevalence of clitoral adhesions in women presenting to the sexual medicine practice*. Journal of Sexual Medicine. Volume 14, Issue 4, Supplement, Page e110.

[141] Related by Abū Dāwūd (no. 5271) and declared ṣaḥīḥ by al-Albānī.

the clitoris, that is reduced in size according to what is appropriate. From these scholars are **Ibn Ḥajar al-ʿAsqalānī**, (d. 1449) **Abū al-Ḥasan al-Mawardī** (d. 1058), **Ibn Taymiyyah** (d. 1328) and **Ibn al-Qayyim** (d. 1350) by way of example. This procedure is to be undertaken by an experienced specialist as indicated by Muslim scholars and Ibn al-Qayyim also discusses the issue of compensation for malpractice.[142]

Fourth: The positive effects and outcomes of this procedure on sexual health are documented in the research literature.[143] They can be summarised in three things: **purity and hygiene, beautifying the appearance of the female sexual organ** and **sexual satisfaction.** Collectively, these affairs lead to a stronger relationship between the husband and wife. However, these affairs are secondary to the fact that circumcision is an act of worship that is pleasing to God.

Fifth: After mentioning that circumcision is a symbol of believers in God and a form of beautification which adds to their internal and external beauty and purity, the Islāmic scholar **Ibn al-Qayyim** (d. 1350) explains: "And what beautification is better than reducing that from the skin of the prepuce (qulfah) that has exceeded the limit in its length... And alongside this, circumcision comprises **purity**, **cleanliness**, **adornment** and **beautification of form (appearance)**, and **regulation of sexual desire**... You will find that uncircumcised men and women are not satiated by sexual intercourse."[144] An excess of the prepuce can hinder stimulation

---

[142] Refer to *Tuḥfat al-Mawdūd* (Jeddah: Majmaʿ al-Fiqh al-Islāmī), p. 283.

[143] Refer to: Placik, Otto J. et al. *A Prospective Evaluation of Female External Genitalia Sensitivity to Pressure following Labia Minora Reduction and Clitoral Hood Reduction.* Plastic and Reconstructive Surgery: October 2015, Vol. 136, Issue 4, pP. 442e–452e. Presenting their results, the authors stated: "At 6 months, an increase in the number of sexual relations was observed in 44.1 percent of subjects ($p = 0.011$), an improvement in orgasm frequency was exhibited by 35.3 percent of subjects ($p = 0.013$), and an increase in orgasm strength was observed in 35.3 percent of subjects ($p = 0.006$)." They also concluded that this procedure does not lead to any loss in genitalia sensitivity. Similar results were demonstrated in a much larger study by Alter GJ in *Aesthetic labia minora and clitoral hood reduction using extended central wedge resection.* Plastic and Reconstructive Surgery. 2008;122:1780–1789. They reported a significant improvement in self-esteem and sex life among the patients.

[144] Refer *to Tuḥfat al-Mawdūd* (Jeddah: Majmaʿ al-Fiqh al-Islāmī), p. 274.

and gratification. Circumcision by a competent practitioner helps resolve this problem and helps regulate sexual desire by enhancing the gratification of the woman which—*as well as pleasing the man*—does not leave her in want due to lack of fulfilment.

Sixth: The National Health Service (NHS) in the UK provides information on **Labiaplasty (vulval surgery)**, stating: "A labiaplasty is surgery to reduce the size of the labia minora—the flaps of skin either side of the vaginal opening. Some women consider having a labiaplasty because they don't like the look of their labia, or because the labia cause discomfort. This is a major decision you should weigh up carefully."[145] After providing details about the cost and the process, they make a careful distinction between this procedure and "female genital mutilation". As has preceded from the speech of Ibn al-Qayyim, adornment and beautification can be considered to be among the aims and benefits of circumcision. Hence, this type of "female circumcision" with empirically verified and proven medical benefits is a highly-beneficial procedure when carried out by **a competent, certified specialist.**

It is clear from the above that confusion is spread regarding this issue by detractors of Islām and in particular, feminists. They do not distinguish between a known medical procedure, *clitoral unhoooding*, and the harmful practice referred to today as "*female genital mutilation*" which originates in ancient African culture. While there are many doubts raised about women in Islām, these specifically chosen examples should be enough inform the reader that the Islāmic legislation—in whatever it obligates, commends or permits—comprises wisdoms and lofty objectives and that it is deeper in sophistication than its detractors may presume. The bias, shallowness in intellect and ignorance of such people are clear to the people of knowledge and erudition in Islām. This brings us to the end of our brief journey into the basics of Islām.

---

[145] Refer to https://www.nhs.uk in the Health section dealing with cosmetic procedures. **Note:** In UK law, "female genital mutilation" is defined as *the partial or total removal of the external female genitalia for non-medical reasons*. It is a criminal, punishable offence in the UK to "*excise, infibulate or otherwise mutilate the whole or any part of a girl's labia majora, labia minora or clitoris*" as stated in the Female Genital Mutilation Act 2003.

Closing Notes

This has been a short and concise primer on Islām and is by no means a comprehensive treatment. It has dealt with only some of the most pertinent issues that Muslims feel the need to clarify and explain. The reader is encouraged to pursue further studies into Islāmic belief, practice and law for further insight whilst being aware that there are ideological and political orientations that spread deliberate misinformation about Islām in order to hinder people from listening to Muslims clarify their beliefs and practices.

Some of them are part of are **well funded networks**— to the tune of tens of millions of dollars—and they have an extremely wide reach.[146] Some of them are **media-savvy trained actors**, using the power of social media to spread propaganda. Some of them have found **tremendous riches** in **peddling hatred** of Muslims by **manipulating and commercialising** the sentiments of millions of citizens of Western nations who are understandably worried about **immigration**, **crime** and **terrorism**. Far-right movements with hidden or subtle racist undertones—aggrieved by immigration and crime—try to blame their woes on Islām and Muslims. They use sophisticated emotional propaganda coupled with a deeply polemical and extremely biased study of Islām that involves frequent lies and distortions. They are sometimes **co-opted** or **given tactical and financial assistance** by others who see their own agendas being advanced in the process.[147]

Because of these sad realities, it is upon the sincere person to be cautious and diligent regarding claims that are brandished about Islām and Muslims, especially those which are deeply polemical and used for hatemongering.

---

[146] Refer to: "*The Cold War on British Muslims. An examination of Policy Exchange and the Centre for Social Cohesion*" available on http://www.spinwatch.org. Also: "*Fear Inc. The Roots of the Islamophobia Network in America*", available on the website http://www.americanprogress.org, an investigation conducted by the Center for American Progress Action Fund revealing a small, tightly networked group of misinformation experts guiding efforts reaches millions of Americans through advocates, media partners, and grassroots organising.

[147] A clear example of this is the collusion between ultra-Zionists from the US, Canada and Australia with the likes of Tommy Robinson and the EDL.

How to Become a Muslim

Entering into Islām is simple and easy.

A person enters into Islām by verbally expressing the following statement, known as the *shahādah*, with full knowledge, conviction, truthfulness and utmost sincerity:

Ash-hadu allā ilāha illalāh. Wa ash-hadu anna muḥammadan ʿabduhu wa rasūluh.

The explanatory meaning of this statement is:

"I testify that none has the right to be worshipped except Allāh alone—[the God of Abraham, Moses and Jesus]—and I testify that Muḥammad (ﷺ) is His slave and messenger."

When you utter this statement aloud you have entered into Islām. Although witnesses are not necessary for your entry into Islām to be valid and acceptable to Allāh, it is recommended to express this statement in front of other Muslims. Preferably, in the presence of someone who is learned as they will be able to instruct you further. As for taking a bath after you have entered into Islām, it is not an obligation, though you may do so if you wish.

Upon entry into Islām all of your past sins—*no matter what level they reached*—are forgiven by Allāh. He is the Most-Merciful and forgives on account of grace and mercy, without requiring *blood-sacrifices*, *tribal memberships* and *special genes*. The Prophet (ﷺ) said: "*Islām wipes away all of your past sins.*"[148]

Allāh continues forgiving the sins of His believing servants so long as they do not knowingly and stubbornly persist in these sins and are sincere in their repentance. As a former non-Muslim, you may have habits and influences from your past that may take time to relinquish. They can be best overcome by focusing on **the most important things first**, which are the pillars and major obligations. This will allow you to build a firm foundation from which you can then proceed to tackle those other issues more easily.

If you have just become a Muslim, then welcome! May Allāh bless you and grant you the best of this life and the next.

---

[148] Reported by Muslim in his Ṣaḥīḥ (no. 121).

Notes

Notes